WHY WOMEN NEED QUOTAS

PROVOCATIONS

WHY WOMEN NEED QUOTAS

VICKY PRYCE

WITH RESEARCH BY
STEFAN STERN

SERIES EDITOR:
YASMIN ALIBHAI-BROWN

Biteback Publishing

First published in Great Britain in 2015 by
Biteback Publishing Ltd
Westminster Tower
3 Albert Embankment
London SE1 7SP
Copyright © Vicky Pryce 2015

ISBN 978-1-84954-786-4

10 9 8 7 6 5 4 3 2 1

A CIP catalogue record for this book is available from the British Library.

Set in Stempel Garamond

Printed and bound in Great Britain by
CPI Group (UK) Ltd, Croydon CR0 4YY

Contents

Part I

Part I

My Story

My story

'But we've even had a woman prime minister!
How bad can it be, really?'

MRS THATCHER CAME and went. A truly significant person. But twenty-five years after her fall, and almost two years after her death, women are dissatisfied, and rightly so. We have been patient. We have been nice. We have tried persuasion. We have given businesses and organisations the benefit of the doubt.

No longer. I will argue in this book that the time has come to introduce mandatory quotas into workplaces to ensure that women can at last have a fair chance to get on. Quotas will bring an end to the terrible waste of talent, and the gross economic inefficiency, that we see today.

Some people do not like quotas. There are principled objections, which I shall consider in this essay. But you may as well know my conclusion now: they are the only way to make serious and lasting progress. In the following pages I shall set out why.

Despite having a woman as head of state, the blunt truth is that Britain is a women-unfriendly country. We are slipping behind in the world gender equality league tables despite protestations to the contrary. This year the World Economic Forum rankings of gender equal societies had us in twenty-sixth place, down from eighteenth place a year ago. This puts us behind fourteen European countries, as well as the United States, Rwanda and Nicaragua.[1] The main reason we were pushed out of the top twenty for the first time ever was that we scored comparatively poorly in terms of pay differentials and promotion prospects with men. We also scored poorly on the numbers of women in Parliament, the government and on company boards.

---

1 Rosemary Bennett, 'Women workers get fairer deal in Rwanda than the UK', *The Times*, 28 October 2014.

This book is about economics and the dreadful waste in the labour market thanks to anti-women policy and practice by employers, to which successive governments have turned a blind eye. This book is not intended to be a whinge about how hard women find it getting a fair deal and reaching the top – but instead it is meant to look at the evidence of *how* society is operating these days and explore *why* women find it hard, *whether* discrimination still exists and *what* the benefits might be if that were eliminated. It is a question of lost talent and opportunity, which costs the economy dear.

Estimates by the Equality and Human Rights Commission suggest that there are 5,400 women 'missing' from the top jobs in the UK and that, though there has been a narrowing of the gender gap across business, politics and the media, this has been 'tortuously slow'. Looking back over ten years shows that progress has been poor and that in some sectors we have in fact seen a slowing down and even gone backwards.[2] According

---

2   http://www.theguardian.com/local-government-network/2011/sep/13/few-women-local-government-jobs, accessed 2 February 2015.

to the EHRC report 'Sex and Power 2011', on average since 2003 women held just 10.2 per cent of all senior posts in business, 15.1 per cent in media and culture, 26.2 per cent in politics and even in what is meant to be a diversity-conscious public sector just 26.1 per cent.[3] That can hardly be a sustainable or desirable situation.

An unusual upbringing

I was first encouraged to think about the weirdness of women being treated differently from men while I was growing up in Greece in the late '60s. My mother, despite being a enthusiastic mathematician, was prevented by her father and five brothers from going to university to study physics. This just wasn't done. Sending a girl to spend all her time with men in university – what would the neighbours think? Today we see this sort of attitude in Afghanistan and many other less developed countries, especially those where religion dominates politics. But

---

3   http://www.equalityhumanrights.com/sites/default/files/documents/
     sex+power/sex_and_power_2011_gb__2_.pdf, accessed 2 February 2015.

in post-war Europe not so long ago, similar attitudes prevailed. This was especially true in countries where religious beliefs were strongly held. Until all faiths allow women the same right to be preachers and priests or imams, women will always be held back.

So instead, thwarted by her family, my mother, this very clever but frustrated woman, pursued other interests. She was the best electrician and mechanic anyone ever met. She fixed everything in our house and those of myriad relatives. This was an unpaid hobby. She also became an expert poker player, financing all her expenses and many of ours through her gains over the years. She rode a motorbike, wore leather jackets, smoked while my father wasn't watching and was wonderfully unconventional for her time. She also believed in all of us, her son and daughters, having similar opportunities, and though Greece was still a very prudish country, she had no problem with us mixing freely with members of the other sex. She commandeered a spot next to our summer house and turned it into a volleyball ground where everyone from the neighbourhood would get together and play every afternoon – and so it was that my younger sister became a professional with the top volleyball team in Greece and was on the national team for years thereafter.

But mixing with boys was so frowned upon by the rest of our enormous family of uncles and aunts and many cousins (my father was one of ten, my mother one of seven) that my female cousins were forbidden to come and stay with us because there were boys around. 'Boys?' I used to think. 'What is so special about them? And if boys can go wherever they want, why can't girls?' Interestingly, this freedom was not extended to all aspects of our lives. My father was concerned, when I was in my early teens, that I would be seen by neighbours going out with boys on my own, even though I was in a mixed school. Appearances had to be kept up.

However, in this mix of confused values it was perfectly OK to go out partying from a very young age as long as my brother was with me! So my brother and I perfected a solution. His friends liked to really party; my friends, who in fact were his own schoolmates, liked more sober pastimes – classical music and chess. We would therefore get ready to leave together, say our goodbyes to our parents, exit the house and, after a few hundred yards, separate and go our own way. We would then meet, each agree on a story and return home together. It worked a treat, but it infuriated me deep down: why were women so restricted and not men? And why did my brother, useless as far as I was concerned, who never did any work at school and got away with it, automatically have such a right that I had to fight for? It was incomprehensible to me. Perhaps this was the first stirring of feminism inside a young Greek girl.

Educating Vicky

My parents were, however, very keen on our education. My mother forbade us all from playing the piano as it was a waste of time. She had learned to play it as a young girl, she would often tell us, 'and see where it got me. Nowhere!' Instead, she taught us all maths and insisted that the time we would spend playing the piano could be more usefully spent learning languages. In retrospect I suspect we could have done both but she was adamant, although there was a piano in the house. We all learned more than one language. We learned French as toddlers and my brother and sister went to the American schools for boys and girls respectively.

I was sent to the German School of Athens. I count my blessings to this day. I was the only one who finished school early enough to have exclusive lunch with my parents every day, dictating in the morning what I wanted to eat. This private audience allowed me to increasingly brainwash my parents about women and their rights; they were gradually capitulating in relation to women in society and becoming even more liberal in their attitudes than before. The German School was a mixed school where girls were in a minority. That helped me hugely. I went into the science stream for the last couple of years, one of the few girls to do so, as I was useless at classics. My best friends were boys. But no real distractions were allowed as my parents would have felt let down if I didn't perform. It was a great incentive to forget your gender and just get on with studying.

Whatever you think of the Greeks these days because of the Eurozone crisis and their role in it, the poor Greek kids are worked very hard, with extra lessons after school happening every day. At the French academy, where I would go in the evenings, my '*Assez-bien*' mark one year was not good enough for my father, who looked terribly disappointed at my mediocre result, so I decided to try slightly harder to get his approval. From then on I was awarded the second prize each year as I progressed. Why only the second one, and with such regularity? I had worked out the minimum effort required to get a '*Très bien*' and a book prize each year. There was no point in striving for perfection, as the effort required would not be commensurate to the reward. Economic rationality at a young age! I had already worked out that the opportunity cost of working that much harder on French was too great – I could do something else useful with my time.

And so to London

And I did. My father, intent on improving our horizons, decided that English had to be the next language to learn. So he hired a tutor and one summer he also sent me to a language school outside Reading to do an intensive course. As luck would have it, the place was packed with French girls, who would put on their 'hot pants', the style of the period, take the train to Paddington and then descend, with wide-eyed me in tow, onto the King's Road, where *everything* was happening. And I fell in love with London, deciding that the idea of studying in Germany no longer appealed.

I had been many times to Germany already, and it was a great country of course, even before re-unification. But London was *hot*. And to me the interesting thing was that, as a girl, I would have fewer restrictions than in Greece. I was astonished that one could wear whatever one wanted whereas Greece was so conventional and you had to conform. And I sensed that the place was so much more open to women than Greece at that time, despite the exceptional liberalism (in most areas, though not all, as I describe) of my parents. I was allowed to start studying for entry exams for the UK (O levels, as they were then, and A levels) and eventually came to the UK just as I turned seventeen. A year later, I went to study at the London School of Economics.

For those readers who think this was just the result of a privileged background, I hasten to add that by that time, Greece had a dictatorship under the colonels who had staged a coup in 1967 and my father's business, which was in tourism, collapsed. Once in London, I had to fend for myself and get employment and then scholarships to study. I have supported myself entirely since my late teens.

I found the UK so much more advanced and so much more open to opportunities, including to foreigners like me, than Greece. But I soon realised that in the actual area of work, things were not that easy. American women who came to work in the City or in law in that period of increasing globalisation were rather surprised at our backwardness in the way women were treated over here. I found myself joining an organisation some of them set up, the City Women Network, and in fact helped in drafting its constitution.

When I first joined the City more than three decades ago as the first female ever to have been employed as an economist at Williams & Glyn's Bank, later the Royal Bank of Scotland, where one of my colleagues in

our Edinburgh office was a very bright young economist called Alex Salmond (yes, the very same!), I fondly
thought that things were bound to change. Well, they
have, but by rather less than I might have hoped or
expected. It is often the case that I will be one of few professional women at City events and when I am asked to
speak at dinners, I may be the only woman in the room.
Of course there are professions where women now pro-
liferate – in media, teaching and so on – but even there
they are still in a minority in senior positions. Recent
studies demonstrate that girls, though bright and dili-
gent, get put off specific subjects, especially scientific
ones, and this is felt down the line. If they do make it
through, then hurdles appear later on, as career-enhanc-
ing, part-time, family-friendly work is often hard to
come by.

Getting on and up – learning lessons

I became manager of the economics office of the bank I
had joined in my mid-twenties. I had taken being one
of very few professional women economists in the

City in my stride, not paying too much attention to how exceptional that was. On being promoted, I then started deputising for my boss, the bank's chief economist and director. He was a brilliant New Zealander near retirement age who had been in the RAF during the war and had spent time in a Japanese prisoner-of-war camp.

He was one of the greatest gentlemen around, with brilliant strategic vision, and was more than keen that I should advance despite being a woman. Most women at that time – and many still now – owed their careers to visionary men. Indeed, Alison Wolf in her book *The XX Factor* argues that women bosses are in fact less willing to help other women come up the ladder. I don't know whether that is universally the case. But I overheard my boss one day on the phone to the Bank of England, asking whether it was OK for me to go instead of him to the monthly Advances Group meeting (where the chief economists of the clearing banks (as we were then known) would be grilled about the latest trends in lending activity), given that I was a woman! I remember too the day I was in fact made a manager of the Economics Office a few years later, going round saying hi and shaking hands with all those working for me. A number of the men, as was common practice then, had page three cut-outs pinned on their partition screens in front of them by their desks. As I introduced myself as their new manager, I also asked them to remove the offending sexist pictures – which they did uncomplainingly. Those pictures never reappeared.

Soon after, I started going to high-powered lunches. I was almost always the only woman and a non-drinker to boot. Drinking was rife at that time but no one forced it on you. On my first invite to such a lunch, I had dressed in my best dark clothes and, as I came out of the lift on the top floor of the bank's City headquarters, I was looking around slightly lost. A very nice man rushed over to me and, seeing my uncertainty, asked: 'Are you looking for the kitchens?'

Stunned, I said, 'No. I am a guest!' I knew never to wear black and white again, and I didn't feel comfortable wearing these colours at an event again until I thought I had acquired enough seniority and gravitas not to be mistaken for a young waitress.

Among my staff at the bank was a lovely Scottish woman who was the librarian. In 1975, I was expecting my first child and she followed my pregnancy and my subsequent return to work after six weeks with a lot of sympathy and support. She declared herself uninterested in children, however – absolutely no way would she contemplate having any – and throughout she reemphasised how happy she was to be childless, a decision she and her husband had made. I thought of all sorts of reasons for this attitude, not least that having a child is an expensive business, as I was rapidly discovering.

Now, of course, data confirms that having children is the defining moment when most of the pay gap appears and starts to widen. Childbearing often means that women either leave work never to return, or take a good few years out before re-entering the labour market, or re-entering part-time. The pay gap then materialises and, on average, is never recovered.

But that wasn't the reason for the bank's librarian being so resolutely against having children. I later discovered that she and her trade union official husband in fact did have a daughter, by then already a fourteen-year-old, but had somehow managed to keep it quiet. When she had had her daughter, being pregnant led to automatic dismissal and there was no equality in law between men and women. So she told no one.

The Equal Pay Act had been passed in 1970 and took some five years to become fully effective. Nevertheless, when I had Child Number 1 in 1975 I still put it down as time off to revise for my master's – which was true: I took my master's six months after she was born and when I was still working full-time. In my case, resigning or taking part-time work was out of the question, as I needed to carry on earning real money. I took just a few weeks off again when my second daughter was born three and a half years later.

Another example of anti-women bias may interest those too young to know the conditions of those times. When I joined the City in 1973, men in the bank where I worked, and in other 'clearing' banks, could borrow on very cheap subsidised mortgages at the age of twenty-one, but women could do so only if they were spinsters or could prove they would have no children – ever! Due to the Equal Pay Act, this was changed to twenty-three for all, and women of all ages and shapes were allowed to borrow. I took full advantage of that and arranged the funding for my first house as soon as I got to that age myself.

Have things changed? Of course. Some of what I describe above could not happen today. But it is still hard to be a woman with ambition and talent. Subtly, quietly, employers bypass anti-discrimination laws and regulations: by simply not hiring women in the first place or failing for whatever unspecified reason to promote them to senior positions. In my stints working for various companies, I have experienced and seen the stereotyping and discrimination women face in all sorts of subtle ways and the negative impact this has on their career paths and eventually their pay and contribution to society. Younger women who should be aiming high are, instead, giving up a lot earlier than one would have thought and lowering their ambitions. The cost to the economy is huge. And the cost to society is even greater. After the life I have had, the struggles and big hopes, I do feel let down. And determined that we need to fight with renewed energy and courage. We must make progress now or possibly we never will.

What good men can do

In the absence of role models, I attribute my career path to three enlightened men who were my bosses early on and who were not fazed at all by the fact that I was female and had children. Two of them were foreign – one from New Zealand, at the bank where I got my first ever job, whom I have already mentioned, and the other Canadian, when I later worked for a major international oil company. The Canadian boss and I shared a secretary. At the time I was a single mother with two children and as I walked into the Mayfair offices in the morning I could see all the men already there – probably since 7.30 – working away. My arrival would be noticed as all doors were ajar – no open plan yet, thankfully, but you still could not pass unnoticed. Then one day my boss called me in and said that it was obvious to everyone that I came in later than all the others. Could I do something and get in earlier from then on? I was shocked, though I should have seen it coming. I replied that I'd love to but I had to do the school run in the mornings. I had no problem in the evenings as I had organised daily help. He was terribly apologetic. It hadn't occurred to him that I had children as we had never discussed it. The matter was never raised again. I carried on with my normal hours. We became great friends and he then came to my second wedding, as did my first boss, the New Zealander.

And then, in 1986, as the oil price was crashing, causing great problems for the oil companies, I went for an interview at a major accounting firm to be their chief economist. The address was Queen Victoria Street. I knew the street well as being the one that connected the Bank of England to Mansion House Tube. In my ten years in the City I had walked around there almost every day. So I got off at Mansion House, not realising that what I knew was only part of the street; in fact, to my horror, the road carried on down a hill for at least half a mile all the way to Blackfriars Bridge. The number I was looking for was right at the bottom of it and in completely the opposite direction to the one I had been walking in for a while. Suffice to say I arrived at my destination twenty minutes late and entered the office of the partner who would be my boss twenty-five minutes late. By this time I had lost any hope of getting the job. He rose from his desk and said, 'Hello, you must be very well organised.' My heart sank; what a put-down. I managed to mumble, 'What do you mean?' And his reply stunned me: 'To work full-time and have two children!' I had managed to stumble across a rare man who valued that in an employee. I knew then I had got the job. And I stayed and became a partner there four years later. I owe it all to that inspirational man, the third one to have helped my career along.

I carried on working full-time as Child Number 3, then Child Number 4 and finally Child Number 5, as I used to refer to them, came along. But you can take your commitment to the job too far. There was one time I came back from a trip in the Middle East – I was then partner in charge of International Privatisations at KPMG. It was summer, a hot day, the crescent where I live was having a Pimm's and juice party. All the neighbours, kids, including mine with the au pair, dogs etc. were outside in the garden in the middle of the grove enjoying the fine weather and having a great time. My taxi pulled in and I got out in front of my house and, in full view of everyone, Child Number 4, five years old at the time, saw me and started running excitedly towards me with arms outstretched ready for an embrace, shouting at the top of her voice, clearly heard by everyone, 'Daddy, Daddy, Daddy, Daddyyy!!!' I didn't quite know where to look. That was some confused child…

There was another time when I was working late in the office, something my au pair was quite used to, and I rang to check how things were. One of the kids picked up the house phone and put me on loudspeaker. I couldn't quite understand what was going on as there was a lot of noise in the background. I am quite a strict mother and I asked, rather annoyed, what on earth was going on. 'But Mum,' came the answer, 'it is [my youngest boy's] birthday!' Well – I will never forget that incident. It was a sobering experience. There was a party scheduled for the weekend for his nursery friends, but, as usual, children from the neighbourhood and grandparents had turned up on the actual birthday itself to see him – and I had completely forgotten the date! I rushed home feeling the mother of all guilts! And my children have never let me forget it, in the nicest possible way. It has become a standard family joke and a sketch regularly performed with great hilarity at Christmas by the kids.

But you can't always be there. I got a call on my mobile one afternoon from the head of sports in my daughter's junior school to say that as she was captaining the netball team my daughter could not be picked up at the normal time. Could I please go and collect her an hour later after the match they were due to play? I was stunned to be rung up as they normally ring the house rather than my mobile. I had never spoken to that lady before. I had just come out of a business meeting and had made arrangements for my au pair to collect the kids from school. 'But I am in Bangladesh,' I answered shakily – which was indeed the case! Schools assume that mothers are just doing flower-arranging at home and are available as a child taxi service all during the day. Schools hardly ever phone the father at work and expect him to drop everything if a child has a problem.

Ah, children and their impact! I remember being very heavily pregnant with Child Number 5 shortly after being made a partner – the first mainstream consultancy female partner at the major accounting firm I worked for. We were due to present to a big UK bank and, I kid you not, the banking partner at the firm was raising objections to me going to present our economic predictions because he worried about the reaction of the client to a very heavily pregnant woman 'lecturing' them. It is true I was huge – my last child broke the hospital records for size when he was born. But in the end I did it and it went well.

The pregnancy, though, probably did affect the path of my future career. During that same period – the Thatcher years – I was meant to front an early privatisation bid and was the partner who would be in charge of this huge proposal to the Treasury and the Department of Trade and Industry. I had done all the preliminary work and put the bid together, working with our corporate finance people. Well, as luck would have it, the day of the bid presentation was also the day I was supposed to give birth to my son. The public sector client team we were presenting to didn't seem to mind at all what state I was in and were prepared to put up with me not being there on the day. But my firm believed that the person in charge should always be at the presentation, as they were – and would be – the most important contact for the client during the assignment. A lot of murmurings went on, even suggestions that perhaps I should try to have the baby earlier to guarantee I was going to be fit and available on the day. And, in the end, the senior partners decided that there was too much at stake and they couldn't take the risk. So someone else, a great guy for whom I have a lot of respect, was assigned the role of lead partner and I was moved to a subordinate role, just dealing with the economic aspects of the privatisation process.

Well, I did produce my son on the due date, a Tuesday. The team went, and told the client that if we won, the whole team, including me, as I had been the most visible person while the bid was being prepared, would be at the first meeting. We won it. So three days after giving birth, I rolled out of bed, put working clothes on (well – whatever fitted at the time – not a great choice…) and made it to the meeting in Whitehall. It got me back to work much quicker than when I had had any of the previous children. The other partner who took over was made, on the back of it, head of corporate finance, one of the most coveted senior jobs in the firm. His successor as head of corporate finance went on to become head of the whole firm.

In my early days in the City, the women who got on were those who were unmarried or had no children. Sadly, to make their mark, it seemed to me that they were expected by a male-dominated profession to behave like a man before they were accepted. Have things changed? Maybe. But have we really moved very far? The short summary of the recent, very welcome, appointment of Inga Beale as the first woman head of Lloyd's of London on *The Times* front page read: 'An unmarried former rugby player has smashed through the glass ceiling to become the first woman head of Lloyd's of London.'

This kind of boorish news writing can only come from men. I met Inga Beale at a private dinner organised by the Lord Mayor soon after – the Lord Mayor then being a woman herself – and rugby is the last thing that enters your head when you meet her. What about the formidable skills and experience that she brought to the role? The headline somehow forgot to mention those.

What I have tried to do in this book is draw on available economic data from the UK and elsewhere as well as accounts of the experiences of successful women. I and my co-writer Stefan Stern have also carried out a series of selective interviews with a number of high-profile women, as well as some men, in politics, business and academia. What we wanted to do was understand what has helped and what may have hindered progress, what have been the personal issues women have faced as they've moved up the career ladder, how much their environment has influenced their own attitudes and those of others around them, and how they have perhaps fought against it. We also delved into the way they are treated by the media, which puts many women off the idea of seeking high position, and the ensuing loss of privacy and impact on family life, and tried to discern any changing trends. We spoke to many in the younger generations, including my three daughters and their friends, to see what they thought of the opportunities and obstacles they had to deal with as they were embarking on their careers.

Some of the questions we asked in relation to women in businesses and across all other areas of public life were meant to allow us to get to the bottom, if we could, of issues such as:

- Who's got to the top, how and why?

- Do women make better bosses?

- Why haven't more women got to the top?

- Is anything really changing?

- Is there a need for 'positive discrimination'?

- Is there a problem with culture?

- Is there an absence of role models?

- What needs to be done?

Part II

What's holding women
back – the evidence

Part

T

What's holding women back – the evidence

THINKING BACK TO my own experience, I realise that at the time I started, I was being a bit of a pioneer, but I thought future generations of women would find it much easier. I was wrong. We celebrate some successes. But it seems to me from the evidence Stefan Stern and I have gathered that younger women today face almost as many and in some ways additional challenges to the ones I faced, which make it still very difficult to penetrate many areas of male dominance. How else do you explain the fact that although more girls than boys get the best educational results, including in medicine, hardly any heads of hospital trusts are women, and a very small number of women are top consultants or chief executives? Professional occupations, which are more highly paid, are being increasingly penetrated by women and that helps generally reduce the overall pay gap. But even here, the pay gap for health professionals remains a high 15.4 per cent. Women, who enter academia in droves, still make up only 20 per cent of professorships and even fewer are heads of department. A tweet from the Times Educational Supplement on 18 November 2014 made a very strong point by saying simply: '78 per cent of professors, 72 per cent of senior managers and 81 per cent of vice-chancellors in the UK are … men'. In the legal profession, where women represent the majority (62 per cent) of those entering the trade, less than a third are partners. The twenty top-paid athletes in the world, listed in an article that appeared just before Christmas 2014, contains no females at all and it is still acceptable in many sports to pay women a fraction of what the men get, even though they may compete in as many tournaments in the year as the men – Grand Slam tennis tournaments now being the honourable exception.

In film, the discrepancy is enormous – data for 2012 suggests that women directed only 9 per cent of the top-grossing Hollywood films in that year.

The issue, therefore, will be to explore what change, if any, is needed to create a stronger, richer and more just society and economy. Would quotas, not just on boards – resisted by many – be justified or make a difference?

The corridors of power and influence

The evidence suggests that women now outperform men in educational achievement. Figures recently published by UCAS, the universities and colleges admissions service, showed that women are a third more likely to enter higher education than men. Among eighteen-year-olds, 34 per cent of women were allocated university places, compared with 26 per cent of men, the widest this gap has ever been. Put another way, four out of every seven higher education places are now going to women.

Yet the fact is that women are still very badly underrepresented at the top in most walks of life. Even today,

93 per cent of executive directors are men and 77 per cent of Parliament is male.

Let's start with big business and the issue of women on company boards, which is an important focus for the book though by no means the only one.

Change has taken place, but slowly. Mervyn Davies's review in 2011 was an attempt to accelerate female representation on the boards of FTSE-listed companies using a voluntary approach. Companies could set their own targets but there was a bottom line. By the end of 2015, FTSE 100 companies should have at least 25 per cent female representation on their board. He estimated that this would require one-third of all new board positions to be taken by women.

The latest monitoring report from Cranfield University, produced in March 2014, found that thirty-six of the FTSE 100 had 25 per cent or more female representation on their board and concluded that, at this rate of progress, 25 per cent of FTSE 100 directors would be female by the end of 2015. A Department for Business, Innovation & Skills (BIS) report in October 2014 found that progress has continued. The percentage of directors of FTSE 100 companies who were female had gone up from 20.7 per cent in March to 22.8 per cent. This compared favourably with 17.3 per cent in April 2013 and just 12.5 per cent when Davies launched his report in 2011.[4]

But, individually, many firms are way below this target – 61 per cent of FTSE 100 firms were still below the 25 per cent at that stage and, among the FTSE 250, women's representation in the boardrooms is only just over 17 per cent. As Lord Davies put it in a *Guardian* article:

> Having reached a position where it is unacceptable for the voice of women to be absent from the boardroom, it is disappointing to see there are still 29 all-male boards in the FTSE 250. Every single company needs to address the issue of gender balance in the boardroom and make sure they support UK business in our collective goal.[5]

---

4   Simon Goodley, '60 per cent of Britain's firms still to reach government target for female directors', *The Guardian*, 9 October 2014.

5   Ibid.

There is no doubt that many are trying, though often starting from a very low base. The eleventh edition of 'Movers & Shakers', published in late November 2014 by Sapphire Partners, an executive selection firm specialising in women executives and non-executive directors for boards, showed that 164 female board and executive appointments were made over the previous three months, predominantly within the FTSE 100 and FTSE 250, but also in roles outside the UK.[6]

Over the previous twelve months the number of women appointed to non-executive director (NED) and executive positions in the FTSE 100 and FTSE 250, as well as professional services and the not-for-profit sector, was a healthy 563. At the same time, though, some 135 women left senior roles, making it a net gain of just 428. At least it suggests that there is, as the research highlights, 'a growing female talent pipeline of potential chairs, CEOs and NEDs' to look forward to. The 48 per cent increase in female executive positions across all companies in the most recent quarter covered by the

---

6 Sapphire Partners, 'Movers & Shakers', Quarterly Report, November 2014.

Sapphire Partners report (a total of ninety-three, set against sixty-three in the prior quarter) is also welcome. Of those, forty-one appointments were in financial services, twenty-five in other non-financial firms, twenty in professional services and seven in the not-for-profit and charity sector.

Non-executive directors: pros and cons

Any increase in female representation is to be welcomed, of course, and is clearly good news. But on closer examination, the data reveals the limitations of a voluntary approach. The truth is that in practice, this has hardly made a dent to the overall male dominance. Women hold just 6.9 per cent of executive positions across the board, and the pace of change is slow – in 2009, it was 5.2 per cent. Hardly a major shift. As of November 2014, just five blue-chip companies were run by women.[7] This comes after Kingfisher appointed insider Véronique Laury as CEO. And the overall increase in

---

7   Serina Sandhu, *Independent on Sunday*, 28 September 2014.

female representation in senior roles across the various categories has come about almost entirely from more women taking non-executive directorships. In practice, many companies have achieved their 25 per cent female board ambition largely on the basis of picking the low-hanging fruit: in other words, by recruiting more women from the outside, often from outside the UK, to serve as non-executive directors rather than having more high-ranking female executives from within their organisations joining the board. Indeed, the BIS October 2014 report showed that executive female directors represented on FTSE 100 boards were a mere 8.4 per cent. The overall figure of 22.4 per cent women on boards was boosted by an increase in part-time non-exec roles, with the number of female NEDs rising to 27.9 per cent.[8]

And often the selection of those NEDs is from a relatively small band of women who hold multiple NED positions on many company boards at the same time. Even if that doesn't worry you, then what might is the

8   Simon Goodley, '60 per cent of Britain's firms still to reach government target for female directors', *The Guardian*, 9 October 2014.

evidence in the November 2014 'Movers & Shakers' report of a 35 per cent decline in the most recent quarter for which they had data in the number of female NED appointments (fifty, compared with seventy-seven in the prior quarter). More alarming was a 20 per cent drop in women appointed to their first plc NED roles. This is often a Catch-22 for women who lack previous experience at that level, as this was a traditionally male enclave – Grayson Perry's middle-class, middle-aged, white 'default man' – and women therefore have more of a hurdle to overcome than many a man.

So even if the 2015 target is met, in many ways that is relatively insignificant as it is the executive senior posts that make a difference to the culture of the organisation, not some board meetings no one gets to know much about. Although there probably is more mileage in appointing more women to non-executive roles, developing the talent pipeline for executives is harder to solve and will take longer. But it is much more important. That is where the market failure is more pronounced, as the externalities (spillovers) are considerably larger: executives decide what the big problems are and formulate the options for solving them; at best, non-executives advise on the choice of options. So this is where change is needed most of all.

A new initiative to increase the number of women in CEO positions, '25 by 25', has been launched by Moya Greene, the Royal Mail CEO. This is a more ambitious target, as it relies on CEO appointments and would mean that, over the next decade, one in six new CEOs appointed would need to be female. This more organic initiative has been heavily encouraged by the Business Secretary Vince Cable, who launched a 'gold standard award' to those recruitment firms who have done the most work to support the appointment of women to FTSE 350 companies. Miranda Pode, the UK managing director of Egon Zehnder, the executive headhunting firm, said that she hoped the initiative would act as a catalyst for realising the potential of women whose 'careers might follow different trajectories to those of their male counterparts' because they take career breaks. And since two-thirds of chief executive positions are recruited internally, Egon Zehnder is helping firms prepare and encourage women internally for such opportunities, by assisting them in identifying those talented female employees with leadership potential, launching leadership development programmes and, more directly, discussing with individual women their career aspirations and development plans.

Current options and comparisons

UK companies can often cope with skill deficiencies in their workforce by recruiting from abroad, but this is not really an option when it comes to recruiting more women executives. Female under-representation is a problem everywhere and businesses in most countries are under pressure – sometimes backed by law – to do something about it.

Working out how different countries compare is not straightforward because of differences in corporate governance requirements as well as in the population of businesses being considered. The Davies Review used 2009 data produced by Governance Metrics International (published as an annex to the report). At that time, the estimate for the UK was 7.8 per cent women on boards – this refers to a wider population of businesses than the FTSE 350, so the figure can't be compared with the 25 per cent Davies target. In Europe, the Nordic countries were head and shoulders above the rest, with Norway having 35.9 per cent female representation, Sweden 23 per cent and Finland 21 per cent. But the UK was just behind Germany (9 per cent) and France (8.2 per cent). Companies were also doing better in the USA (11.4 per cent), New Zealand (11.4 per cent), Canada (11.3 per cent) and Australia (9.9 per cent) – 'Anglo-Saxon' comparators with similar systems of corporate governance, business cultures and preferences for voluntary action rather than state regulation.

There has been progress since 2009, especially in larger companies. Egon Zehnder conduct a regular survey of the 1,000 leading global firms and their 2014 report found that the seventy UK companies in the sample had an average 22.3 per cent female representation. The Nordic countries were still ahead, as was France (28.5 per cent), but in this sample the UK was joint fourth with Australia and ahead of the USA, Canada and Germany.

There are whole areas of investment banking or insurance, such as underwriting, where women are virtually non-existent, and if they are there at all, they are token women. In politics, this is now becoming a defining issue for the various parties, with the Conservatives being attacked about the lack of female candidates, Labour being slightly more progressive due to all-women shortlists, and the Lib Dems likely to lose most of their women MPs in the next election. When I started putting thoughts together for this book, there were no women members of the Monetary Policy Committee or the Financial Policy Committee; there is now one female internal member on both – one of the Bank's deputy governors, Manush Shafik, who joined recently from the IMF. But there is still just one external member on any of the committees: Kristin Forbes, who joined the MPC last year, though she had to be imported from the US. And there are still only five female FTSE 100 chief executives and only one woman chair of a FTSE company – and this in 2015.

Women fought hard to get a female on the English bank notes when, for some reason, Mervyn King, then

Bank of England Governor, decided to drop the prison reform campaigner Elizabeth Fry, the only well-known English woman honoured in this way, to make room for Winston Churchill. At least now the £10 notes will have Jane Austen on them from 2017, but the campaign to make that happen resulted in Caroline Criado-Perez, a journalist who was a prominent supporter of the campaign, being viciously attacked on Twitter and the internet and there were threats on her life. She told HuffPost UK in the summer of 2013:

> For me, the really shocking thing is how this has happened over such a tiny, tiny thing. We asked for there to be a woman on a bank note, how does asking that even annoy someone? Annoy someone so much they send a barrage of rape threats? It's kinda gobsmacking … it's not about what women are doing, not about feminism. It's that some men don't like women, and don't like women in the public domain.[9]

---

9   http://www.huffingtonpost.co.uk/2013/07/27/twitter-rape-abuse_n_3663904.html, accessed 2 February 2015.

Countless articles recently are highlighting the need to push harder in this area.

The pay gap between men and women, though generally on a declining trend, is still too high. Figures for the year to April 2014 show that the gender gap for those in full-time employment, measured by average hourly earnings, is still stubbornly around 10 per cent. Although it has almost disappeared at entry level, it develops when people reach their thirties, and widens dramatically when they hit their forties. The gap of average hourly pay for all employees, in both full- and part-time employment, was standing at some 19.1 per cent. The Equality and Human Rights Commission, however, has estimated that the difference overall between mean hourly earnings of men who work full-time and women who work part-time, though declining, was at some 34.5 per cent in 2010 – and this matters, as only 57 per cent of women work full-time, compared with 86 per cent of men.

At a recent Westminster and Industry Group conference on gender equality, where I spoke along with others, the senior women agonised about whether

quotas were a good or a bad thing. But in private dis-
cussions later, the overwhelming view was that quotas
were needed as progress in gender equality remained
very poor. And not only in business but also in the public sector as a whole, in politics and in all walks of life.
The legal profession was singled out for special criticism,
though there are some honourable exceptions among
law firms. When women leave the workforce, even for
a short period, their wages never recover to where they
would have been had they stayed on. For the economy
as a whole, there is a huge loss of productivity as young
women today still drop out in large numbers, frustrated
with the conditions and attitudes in the workplace once
they have children. It also means that when they re-
enter, often in part-time positions, they work at least
one if not two places below their skill level.

Much more therefore needs to be done. Initiatives
such as the '30 Percent Club', made up, as the name suggests, of companies who have pledged to achieve women
board participation of 30 per cent, are laudable and could
make a difference. Bur progress overall in Britain is very
slow. UK foot-dragging is encouraging the European

Commission's push to legislate in this area. EU directives would not be needed if national legislators took the need for fair treatment of women seriously.

Is it us? Do women's choices and behaviour in part contribute to their disadvantage?

Does it help or hinder women to raise the feminist banner? Well, that raises the issue that there is no common understanding of what feminism is, or what it means to be a feminist.

Karren Brady, recently elevated to the House of Lords as a life peer, quoted Rebecca West in an interview in the *Daily Telegraph* in November 2014, saying, 'I myself have never been able to find out precisely what feminism is: I only know that people call me a feminist whenever I express sentiments that differentiate me from a doormat.' The question was raised because Brady set out how she plans to use her new seat in the House of Lords to 'really make a difference'. She said: 'My intention is to really think about ways legislation can help break down barriers – particularly for equal pay.' Currently, on average, women earn just 80 pence for every pound a man is paid. Brady went on: 'Gender shouldn't be a factor that's taken into account when measuring pay, success or attitude.'

But in 2013, Miley Cyrus (previously fresh-faced and squeaky-clean Disney alumnus, now scantily clad and sexually suggestive pop princess) claimed that she considered herself 'one of the biggest feminists in the world because I tell women not to be scared of anything'. She then corrected herself, saying: 'For me, it's not even that I'm a feminist. I'm for anybody. I'm for everybody, for everything. I don't care what you wanna do in your life, or who you wanna be with, who you wanna love, who you wanna look like.' She also stated in *Cosmopolitan* magazine in December 2013 that 'I'm a feminist in the way that I'm really empowering to women. I'm loud and funny and not typically beautiful.'

Cyrus appears to think that encouraging people to behave in whatever way they want is 'feminism'. In some ways, her provocative dress sense is reclaiming the right to look any way she wishes, while maintaining the right to say no. And yet she uses the fact that she is a woman to gain the upper hand by dressing in a way that is aimed at attracting men.

Karren Brady had an answer here. When asked about the comments of a female contestant on *The Apprentice* who told the other women to wear short skirts as they'd 'sell more', Brady said:

> I defend the right of women to wear whatever they want, including short skirts. But if all you've got is a short skirt you are never going to achieve anything. If you don't have a brain, if you can't communicate, if you don't have a strategy or hard work behind you then it doesn't matter how short your skirt is. It will never be short enough.

Do women on the whole suffer from a lack of confidence (at least relative to men)? Do they need to be more confident?

It is often suggested that, when considering whether to apply for a promotion, women will only apply if they think they have the skills and experience to tick all the boxes, whereas men will tend to give it a shot even if they fall short on one or two criteria. But women are also put off by the system, particularly if there are no other role models. Dame Fiona Woolf said in an interview that when she became her law firm's first female partner, she had to ask for it: 'The senior partner was actually quite surprised I might want a partnership.'[10]

Similarly, women are often seen as more reluctant to seek a pay rise. The issue hit the papers recently when Satya Nadella, the CEO of Microsoft (100,000 employees, of which only a fifth are women), while addressing a conference for women in computing, was asked what advice he would offer to female employees who felt uncomfortable asking for a pay rise. He said that asking for more money was a bad idea, that one should wait to be recognised and that not asking for a rise 'was good karma'. Now, this remark may be one he regrets making, and in a sense it may not have been directed solely at women – the CEO of a huge global company probably

---

10 Nick Curtis, 'Who's afraid of Fiona Woolf?', *Evening Standard*, 11 July 2014.

wants to discourage all its employees from asking for a pay rise! – but it brought in its wake many reminders that men are often more comfortable asking for a pay rise than women, and if you don't ask, you don't get.

The theme is taken up by none other than Janet Street-Porter in her *Daily Mail* column. I can't always say that I agree completely with everything the eminent columnist writes, but in this case I do – completely. She wrote her piece around Nadella urging female workers to trust the system. Janet S-P wonders – wisely, in my view – whether that advice is any good. Men, she says, would not sit still and just wait. Instead, as she puts it, 'They revitalise their CVs, polish up their credentials and embellish their achievements, all in pursuit of another step up the pecking order.' Far too many women, on the other hand, 'are hesitant, remain trapped in jobs for which they are over-qualified or paid beneath their worth'.[11]

This 'confidence gap' may of course also partly

---

11 Janet Street-Porter, 'Why women (even me) are scared to ask for a pay rise', *Daily Mail*, 12 October 2014.

explain the pay gap. Women, in large measure, tend to apply for the things they believe they are qualified to do and thus limit themselves to their comfort zone. Men, on the other hand, often have the arrogance to apply for things that on paper would seem to be beyond their reach – and they don't flinch about it.

A woman I know in her thirties, one of the funniest and most capable reporters for a commercial media network, told me that she was once informed by a senior manager that she 'didn't have the face for being a news anchor on television'. What does that mean? She is blonde and pretty – and certainly much prettier than the males who read the news. And intelligence shines through her.

That really shook her confidence. But at least she knows that when her interviews are shown they are among the most perceptive I have ever heard anyone conduct. She has the knack of getting subtly under the skin of well-known political personalities. They don't notice how far they are being gently pushed and therefore say more than they should, as her manner is quietly reassuring and seductive. And yet she is almost never allowed to be the main presenter of the programme she contributes to. She did complain to me that younger men all around her feel no compunction at going and asking to do it, fully confident that they will be OK. She is amazed by that. Then one day, when I was watching at home, there she was, presenting the news. She was brilliant. She told me afterwards that she had suddenly got the courage to ask, as they were looking for someone to cover for the regular presenter. But why had it taken her so long?

A lack of confidence in the workplace has deep roots, supposedly setting in during our teenage years as a result of being less happy than boys because of things like looks, family life and possessions. I have spoken to many of my children's friends and they confirm all the stereotypes we have in mind!

Young women's lack of confidence in their bodies can lead to a negative body image and eating disorders, of which only the most serious may be diagnosed and treated. In how many cases does a residue of obsession or self-loathing carry through into adult life? Those hard-to-suppress inner 'voices' can hold people back.

Women can also appear to hold themselves back if they think that leadership positions, for whatever reason, are not for them. The writer and consultant Sylvia Ann Hewlett, author of several books and president of the Center for Talent Innovation, cites research carried out by her organisation looking at 'mid-career' women (aged thirty-five to fifty). Women in this group who had not achieved leadership positions were less likely to believe that a leadership position would give them opportunities to flourish and achieve what they wished to achieve than women in the same age group who *had* reached leadership positions. Of course, the shortage of women in leadership positions to act as role models is a very good reason why women in less elevated positions have a different perception of the personal value they would gain from leadership.

Should women seeking to get to the top act like a man would, or should they attempt to get there on their own terms?

In spite of difficult odds, an unforgiving environment,

unsympathetic bosses, a hostile culture and any number of other barriers, brilliant women do succeed in reaching the top. But when they do, it can be on terms set out by men. These women operate in the same way as their male colleagues. There may perhaps be a 'house husband' at home, taking on the majority of domestic and caring responsibilities. Helena Morrissey, immensely successful head of Newton Asset Management, founder of the 30 Percent Club, and mother of nine children, is such an example. That may work for some couples. But in general it is the women who fall back on doing the caring roles in the family when the need arises. I would guess that not many women would be fortunate enough, for example, to be in the position of having a spouse who could drop everything and put their own career on hold like the well-known journalist Jackie Ashley did for nine months to look after her husband, Andrew Marr, who has now successfully overcome the disability left after a stroke in 2013 to return to his regular TV and radio presenter roles. Many others may choose, or feel forced, not to have a family of their own at all.

Indeed, they may also feel that the only way to

succeed is to become 'one of the lads' – mirroring the behaviour of their male colleagues, accepting the prevailing norms, tolerating sexism and thereby doing little for the many other women in their organisation who would prefer to see things change. In doing so, these successful women conform to a male pattern but leave the prevailing orthodoxy and culture unthreatened and undisturbed. The example they set for young women may be discouraging rather than encouraging. Nothing changes, and the exodus of other talented women continues.

Role models and queen bees

We need to see more women getting to the top on their own terms, creating positive role models for young women who, even now, are still worried about the sacrifices they may be asked to make. Indeed, Dame Sally Davies, the Chief Medical Officer for England, talks of the 'Queen Bee Syndrome', where a woman in power treats other women more harshly – 'queen bees preening and enjoying being the only woman'. I must admit that in my career the people who have helped me most have been men, while other women did indeed feel threatened and were often poisonous. It is odd to reflect on this now but their behaviour is understandable. After all, they themselves did not have other female role models to emulate, as they were, in many ways, pioneers in their fields. They had worked hard to get to where they were. To do so in a man's world, they had had to fight even harder than the men. And that is all they knew. So they were harsher than the men in all their dealings – in my observation, they were in fact pretty awful to all their underlings, whether male or female, because they had to be seen as tough.

That sort of role model is no role model at all, and has been responsible for turning women off competing in such an environment. But this is gradually changing as norms of acceptable behaviour are also changing. I made a point of hiring women in the bank – one of my great successes was giving Marian Bell, later a member of the Monetary Policy Committee, her first proper professional job. While joint head of the Government Economic Service, I helped to appoint a large number of women to chief economist jobs across Whitehall departments. I mentor women from the outside and am still a member of various women's networking groups, including the Women Economists Group, economics being an area where women are severely under-represented. Many of the stories I hear are of the absence of role models and I am often asked how to diffuse situations that may become toxic to career development if left unchallenged. What is pleasing is when male bosses recommend to their women employees that they should come to me for mentoring – they must know that I will be looking to ensure their progression as quickly as possible! But it is good in that it suggests that it is their male bosses who have realised that good women need a bit of help every now and then to be encouraged to assert themselves and achieve their potential rather than staying on the sidelines. We need more male bosses to behave similarly.

Yet the lack of sufficient role models is still a barrier to progress. I was recently on a train to Birmingham and, with five minutes to spare before we arrived at New Street Station, a young woman sitting opposite opened up conversation, having recognised me. Within a couple of minutes she asked me to be her mentor, as she was looking for progression to the senior civil service – a minute later, I had agreed! What an amazing way to be 'hired'! We have been meeting and communicating ever since. She doesn't actually need me, I don't think, as she seems to be doing all the right things and will definitely go far, but she uses me as a sanity check and that seems to work well.

Another example where a bit of push was needed was when one of my economic assistants was about to apply to take a year out and complete a master's degree. The department would be paying her fees, as she was a star. But even she had confidence problems and wasn't sure where to apply for her one-year graduate course. I told her she was good enough for the LSE, which she was convinced wouldn't have her. I encouraged her to apply, and of course she got in and has been a great success. She came back to the department for a while and was then poached by one of the main consultancy firms. Her degree helped in that. I had found that lack of confidence astonishing. And we are talking late 2000s here, not decades ago.

But even where women are in senior positions or breaking into formerly male-dominated occupations, they are rarely celebrated. Helena Morrissey, in an interview in the *Evening Standard* in April 2013, quoted Sheryl Sandberg, the chief operating officer of Facebook, as saying at an event they were both at that 'men become more popular as they get more successful whereas for women the opposite is true'. That lack of appropriate role models is a big obstacle for girls' ambitions. Recent research by Girlguiding UK found that over 55 per cent of females aged eleven to twenty-one think there is a lack of female role models.[12] According to Miriam González Durántez, a partner in international law firm Dechert and wife of Deputy Prime Minister Nick Clegg, there are in fact hundreds of thousands of fantastic women role models in the UK, and it is the duty of the women of her generation to do more for the young girls of today. She is supporting the national Inspiring Women campaign, which has already

---

12 http://www.girlguiding.org.uk/pdf/girlsattitudesexploredrolemodels_final.
pdf, accessed 2 February 2015.

signed up three-quarters of state secondary schools and saw 10,000 women in the UK speaking to girls in 2014, increasing to 15,000 women in 2015. The main aim is to introduce girls, first-hand, to a range of jobs and show them that women can have successful careers in areas that are currently male-dominated. Hopefully, this will mean that fewer girls inadvertently make academic choices that rule out certain professions, such as dropping science subjects.

Family life: to have one or not to have one?

As the evidence shows, part of the reason so few women climb to executive positions is down to them taking time off for family commitments. Karoline Vinsrygg, Egon Zehnder's UK head of diversity, was quoted saying that companies should 'have an understanding that at certain times of a woman's life, she may focus less on her career but she has not lost her ambition'. She added that many women find it difficult to return after a break, but that companies should 'help them to integrate when they come back to work', and that allowing more part-time work and different amounts of maternity leave would help more companies retain female employees.

According to Karren Brady: 'Childcare is the biggest problem facing women who want to get back into work. You will not go if you haven't got high-quality, affordable childcare. It's not possible. Something has to be done. It's a really big issue – although it's too late for me.' This was in response to questions about George Osborne's initiative to get 500,000 women back into work by 2016. She continued:

> People ask how I manage. And I think, you'd never ask a male executive how he's bringing up his family. It's naturally assumed he's got a wife doing it for him. So I think if you start to break down the perception of the family dynamic, it's a good thing. After all, women are having babies, we're not having lobotomies.

Things, of course, have moved on over the past three decades but much of the conflict between work and children remains. Women mustn't feel they have to choose

PART II

between a career and a family but, at the same time, they need to accept they cannot be perfect at everything. This is the message of a new book, *Choisissez tout* (*Have It All*), by Nathalie Loiseau, formerly the equivalent of the permanent secretary at the French Foreign Affairs ministry and now head of École Nationale d'Administration (ENA), the administrative school that trains France's governing and business elite. Loiseau has been successful in a world that she describes as 'violent, brutal and archaic'. Having reached the top, she has implemented a 'zero-tolerance' policy towards casual sexism – I'm not sure what she would have made of the page three girls that I found in my early years in the City!

A mother of four sons, she argues that, most of all, women need freedom from the pursuit of perfection. This sometimes comes from within, but it can also be due to the expectations of family, friends, employers, colleagues and, indeed, all of us. In a newspaper interview, when asked whether she ever felt guilty about missing the children's bath time, she replied: 'No. What about the happy look of a child who opens the door and tells you about his exploits, his adventures? He is happy to see you … Precisely because you're not there all the time.' She went on: 'I'm in the habit of telling my children that by not always being at home, at their sides, I've spared them years of psychoanalysis in the future.'

I think this is good advice. Of course one never knows how one's children will turn out and how they will cope with things; my five children all differ hugely from each other in terms of strength, tolerance, temper, confidence etc. but I didn't seek perfection. I never knew their friends' names or those of their friends' mothers, which was at times embarrassing; I delegated the occasional school parents' evening to my older daughters, who listened attentively to the teachers of the younger children in loco parentis; and I have still never baked a cake in my life. My children would have loved me to be perfect but knew I couldn't be – and frankly they would not have gone near any cake I baked as they knew how useless I would be at it. 'What, is she having us on? What's in it?'

A final reflection on this is that some role models may be less effective than others. Sheryl Sandberg of Facebook created quite a stir with her book *Lean In* a couple of years ago. Her message was that women really had to get both a bit smarter and a bit tougher if they wanted to get on at work and try to change the culture from within their organisation. This was not in itself bad advice, as far as it went. And her book made fascinating reading. But her thesis made little allowance for the fact that many businesses and organisations are just so badly designed and run that no sensible woman would ever want to lean further in to them. And succeeding on men's terms can only ever be a limited form of success. Critics declared that Sandberg's book could have been subtitled 'Why You Should Be More Like Me'. A possibility for some of her readers, perhaps, but only a small minority of them.

Money, money, money

A factor common to professions and most paid work is that women are more likely to work part-time. Research quoted by the Fawcett Society suggests that 74 per cent of all part-time work is done by women. Evidence from the Chartered Institute of Personnel and Development (CIPD) suggests that people working part-time have higher job satisfaction than people working full-time, but there are penalties in terms of lower earnings – even adjusting for hours – and lack of career advancement.

Most significantly, the gap between full-time and part-time average hourly wage is as high as 37 per cent. The result is that having children directly results in women, who do most of the part-time work once they start a family, taking a hit in their pay and standing in the labour market.

It seems to make sense, therefore, to look more closely at how the pay gap has moved. Figures from the Office for National Statistics (ONS) suggest that, since 2002, the gender pay gap has narrowed by about a quarter, more women have reached the higher levels of education, and fewer of them face having to move to a lower-paid job when returning to work after having children. Nevertheless, the problems associated with maintaining a career alongside caring remain, including the lack of decent-quality part-time work with real opportunities for advancement.

A special analysis of the 2013 Annual Survey of Hours and Earnings that calculated average hourly earnings (median hourly earnings excluding overtime) for each individual year age group also shows when women fall behind.[13] The average hourly rate of pay for women was highest for those aged twenty-five, whereas for men it was age fifty. Women's average hourly pay increases sharply during their early twenties, starts levelling off in their early thirties, drops appreciably in their late thirties, and then drifts slowly downwards during their forties and fifties (the analysis stops at age fifty-nine).

By contrast, men's average hourly pay moves similarly to women's during their twenties but rises throughout their thirties before reaching a plateau throughout their forties, with a steeper drop during their fifties. Until age thirty-four, the difference in average hourly pay between men and women is always below 10 per cent. It then rockets to 30 per cent by age forty, peaks at 45 per cent at age forty-nine, and has narrowed again to 28 per cent by age fifty-nine. The critical period is the late thirties, when women's average earnings are falling whereas those of men continue to rise.

---

13 'UK wages over the past four decades – 2014', Office for National Statistics, http://www.equalpayportal.co.uk/statistics, accessed 2 February 2015.

In its November 2014 report, the Fawcett Society attributed the substantial variation in the differentials with age to what they term 'the motherhood penalty'. In families where just one parent (usually the father) works full-time, it might be seen as reasonable for the other parent (usually the mother) to do the lion's share of childcare and housework. That does not seem to change much when they get back to work. The report argues that as women find themselves still doing the bulk of the childcare and unpaid household work (currently some 65.5 per cent of all the work despite greater involvement from men in recent years), they therefore tend to return to work part-time if they return at all, at least for a while.[14] According to the report, confirming everything that I have seen and we have been told by the people we have interviewed, part-time work, at least in the private sector, offers reduced access to training and career opportunities and may indeed also result in women taking up less senior and lower-paid

---

14 http://www.popcenter.umd.edu/research/sponsored-events/timeuse-2014/
    tu2014_papers/gershuny_sullivan, accessed 2 February 2015.

roles. And this is not because they have lowered their career ambitions but because of the reality of life and the lack of available opportunities, particularly in senior positions, for well-paid part-time work that still allows for them to be valued and promoted just like everyone else.

One young woman who is a junior lawyer in a City firm told me about the desperately long hours everyone was expected to work in her company and pointed out that the men in senior positions there, i.e. the partners, generally had wives at home who were not working but minding the children, thus giving them, the men, the opportunity to work hard and get on. Yet the firm was a good employer and conscious of wanting the women to remain – their culture simply did not allow for this to happen. And the one senior woman this young lawyer works with had just come back, seriously stressed, after having her third child, though she was herself supported by a stay-at-home husband. The young lawyer talked of the lack of flexible arrangements to allow women to carry on working while starting a family; of the need for help with childcare costs and for more part-time work opportunities in senior positions. Without such arrangements, these women just leave when they approach that point in their lives. Economically, that is catastrophic, as all the training one provides is then wasted.

The legal profession is particularly bad at diversity in comparison to others. Baroness Hale is the most senior female judge in the UK. In 2013 she was voted the fourth most influential woman in the UK by the BBC. She was the first woman to be appointed to the UK's Supreme Court and in an interview in the *Evening Standard* with Rosamund Urwin on 12 December 2014, she spoke of the misogyny in some parts of the profession, saying that progress in boosting the number of women in senior judicial roles remains 'painfully slow'. In earlier interviews she has spoken of the culture of 'unconscious sexism' and when talking to Louisa Peacock of the *Daily Telegraph* on 18 April 2014, she is quoted as saying:

> There are women of my generation who've had to face the fact that some people may judge women's behaviours differently from how they've judged men. They accuse women of being ambitious, as if that was a bad thing, or

of being strident, or opinionated. No thing that a man
is ever criticised for.[15]

In the legal profession, as elsewhere, more thought clearly
needs to be given to a 'business case for diversity', as, once
this is understood, a firm could work hard to overcome
the biases that may be inherent in its operations. The civil
service in general has been way ahead of both the private
sector and the professions, and there is a lot to learn from
best practice. Women make up some 37 per cent of the senior civil service at present.[16] But this is not necessarily the
case across the public sector as a whole, where female senior leaders are considerably less evident. The percentage of
female local council chief executives, for example, though
higher than it used to be, was just 23 per cent in 2011.

It makes no sense to have entry levels where women are
represented at least in equal numbers to men and then to

---

15 http://www.telegraph.co.uk/women/womens-business/10773941/Britains-
    most-senior-female-judge-Baroness-Hale-My-biggest-fear-...-When-am-I-
    going-to-be-found-out.html, accessed 2 February 2015.

16 http://www.independent.co.uk/news/uk/politics/labour-pledges-to-increase-
    women-in-senior-civil-service-posts-9621968.html, accessed 2 February 2015.

end up with serious gaps at the top of many career ladders. This simply means that many firms are losing millions of pounds by investing in the training and education of women who leave when they see limited opportunities for progress. The strategic winners in this scenario are the firms that are open to recruiting those who depart firms where opportunities are limited and thus benefit from the training that rival firms have given their junior staff.

What so often determines whether women are reaching senior posts in many occupations is whether they have family responsibilities. It is still the case – although beginning to be less so now – that relatively few women flourish in very exacting jobs where the agenda is not controlled by them, such as journalism, law and consultancy, and the women who do are far more likely than men to be childless.

Indeed, in my early years I came across many female high achievers in the private sector who were childless and were thus able to devote all the time necessary to the pursuit of top jobs. Nothing wrong with that at all … except that women coming up to a point where they want children start to look around and worry about how they can fit them in and still have a glittering career. They see few role models combining the two with any success in senior posts. More often than not, something gives.

Alison Wolf, Professor at King's College London, outlines the point graphically in her book *The XX Factor*:

> Imagine, for example, that you are offered an excellent new job. To take it you have to relocate ... but you are in a relationship ... Try another one ... you are offered the chance to join a small team working on a new, high-profile project. If it goes well, you have a real chance of promotion ... it also means working not just late, but every weekend in the future. It really is your choice ... Do you – did you – do it? Say yes to either of those choices and right there, if you are a woman, motherhood became significantly less likely.[17]

My own daughter, moving from one high-profile consultancy to another and spending a lot of time away, rang me

---

17   Alison Wolf, *The XX Factor: How Working Women Are Creating A New Society* (Profile Books, 2013), pp. 423.

one day from Chicago to tell me with trepidation, as she thought I would disapprove, that she was quitting because the constant travelling was bad for her relationship. Within two weeks her boyfriend proposed. Two small children later, she is a freelance business process re-designer – hard work, no benefits or paid holidays. But it suits them. For her, the sacrifice of a guaranteed high-paying career was the only way to guarantee that she would have a family.

Being a mother seems to be a clincher in terms of what future to expect for a woman. For the man, being a father brings extra happiness and stability. For the woman, of course there is extra happiness, but also huge increases in stress as most of the childcare and housework stays with them. And then the obstacles to progression seem at a stroke to multiply. According to a Fawcett Society survey, some 23 per cent of women who had recently returned to work from maternity leave felt that their opportunities for promotion were worse as a result.[18] And this applies across the board. Some 55 per cent of

---

18 http://www.fawcettsociety.org.uk/wp-content/uploads/2014/08/The-Changing-Labour-Market-2.pdf, accessed 2 February 2015.

respondents to their survey felt that it in order to progress they had to be working full-time. And, of those,
two in five felt that this was due to senior members of
staff assuming (presumably because of their situation)
that the returning women would no longer want or be
suitable for promotion. This is a very large percentage
of people who feel – and in fact probably are – disadvantaged. Even in the civil service, which is an exemplar
of good practice in this area and where I worked for a
while, young mothers working part-time say that not
being there all the time means that somehow, maybe
unconsciously, you get forgotten when interesting
projects are being given out, and hence overlooked for
praise and for rewards, such as promotions.

Another explanation is that women are over-
represented in low-wage sectors, a phenomenon referred
to as 'occupational segregation'. Recent research by the
ONS showed the extent of this. Women dominate areas
such as 'caring, leisure and other service industries',
where they represent 82 per cent of the workforce; in
'admin and secretarial' they account for 77 per cent of
the total number employed and in 'sales and customer

service' they make up 63 per cent of the total.[19] The extraordinary statistic is that 'sales and customer service' and what are termed 'elementary occupations' accounted for one-third of all females who worked part-time in 2013 earning relatively low median earnings for part-time work of £6.79 and £6.53 per hour, respectively.[20] On the other hand, in science, engineering and technology (SET) industries, men make up 88 per cent of the workforce. Women account for just 6 per cent of professional engineers and 2 per cent of engineering apprentices. In medicine, while 70 per cent of the workforce are women, they make up less than half of doctors and less than a third of hospital bosses.[21]

Indeed, gender bias that pushes women in large numbers towards the lower end of the pay scale is shown in the data of a January 2013 report by the Resolution

---

19 http://www.theguardian.com/money/2013/sep/25/uk-women-lower-paid-work-figures, accessed 2 Februay 2015.

20 'Secondary Analysis of the Gender Pay Gap', Department for Culture, Media & Sport, March 2014.

21 'Engineering and Technology: Skills & Demand in Industry – Annual Survey 2012', The Institute of Engineering and Technology.

Foundation, which found that 62 per cent of workers in the UK who were at the time paid below the Living Wage, set then at £7.65 (now increased to £7.85 in the UK and to £9.15 in London), were women.[22] And their position has been worsening. What has happened in the years since the recession started is that, with the substantial cuts in public sector jobs, where women dominate, many have moved to private sector jobs, but often to low-paid, low-skilled jobs in services, where demand for labour has grown. Although better to have a job than none at all, the pay gap is even greater in the private sector – on average, according to the ONS, some 19.2 per cent compared to 11 per cent in the public sector in 2013. What is more, as the Fawcett Society report outlines, many of the jobs created are zero-hour contracts or part-time or temporary. The report points out that since the start of the crisis in 2008, some 826,000 women have moved into types of work that can be classified as low-paid and, because of their nature, also

---

22 'Beyond the Bottom Line: The Challenges and Opportunities of a Living Wage', Resolution Foundation, January 2013.

rather insecure. At the same time, the number of female workers employed part-time but who would like to be working full-time has nearly doubled to 789,000. Another interesting characteristic of this recovery is that about a third of the increase in employment that we have seen has come from the self-employed, of whom some 371,000 have been women. Figures suggest that since the start of the crisis, earnings for the self-employed have fallen by some 22 per cent in real terms. That is huge in itself. But the more worrying thing is that the loss of incomes for these women is even more pronounced – data suggests that the gender pay gap among the self-employed is as high as 40 per cent.[23]

Women also make up a very small percentage of workers in senior roles. Data from the TUC shows that women account for only 25 per cent of chief executives and senior officials.[24] And when women do make

---

23 http://www.fawcettsociety.org.uk/wp-content/uploads/2014/08/The-Changing-Labour-Market-2.pdf, accessed 2 February 2015.

24 https://www.tuc.org.uk/economic-issues/labour-market/equality-issues/gender-equality/highest-paid-occupations-are-%E2%80%98no-go%E2%80%99, accessed 2 February 2015.

it to the top, they tend to earn less. What shocked me was a reference to a piece of research by the Chartered Management Institute in 2014 that found that female managers aged over forty earn on average 35 per cent less than men of equivalent rank. There are also differences in other areas of compensation. For example, bonuses for the average female director, sitting at £41,956 at the time, were some £12,000 less than what was received by the average male director.

Do men and women have different personality traits? Are their values and priorities different?

Are women from Venus and men from Mars? Are there subtle differences between men and women – we're talking average here – that help to explain gender disparities, even if they do not provide an excuse for them?

According to psychologists Binna and Jo Kandola, alleged differences between men and women are often based on ancient stereotypes that have little or no basis in reality today. Binna Kandola refers to what he calls the 'Yabba Dabba Do!' theory of gender role modelling:

> The idea that *The Flintstones* was a documentary, rather than a cartoon, showing Fred as the hunter-gatherer and Wilma as the nurturer at home … it is unknowable how cavemen and women divided their roles, but we think it is likely they were far more evenly split … In fact, up until the industrial revolution, women performed a wide range of roles inside and outside the home – for example, in the thirteenth century, there were female carpenters and masons.

From *The Flintstones*, it is a short step to a world view that women are always 'caring', and therefore not suited to tough leadership roles, whereas 'masculine' traits, such as being decisive, are more highly valued.

Yet perceptions do not always reflect reality. Some analysts state quite baldly that, taken overall, women display more impressive leadership skills than men. Consultants Jack Zenger and Joseph Folkman wrote in *Forbes* in 2012:

They [women] build better teams; they're more liked and respected as managers; they tend to be able to combine intuitive and logical thinking more seamlessly; they're more aware of the implications of their own and others' actions; and they think more accurately about the resources needed to accomplish a given outcome.

And that was not all that the Zenger and Folkman study uncovered: 'Two of the traits where women outscored men to the highest degree – taking initiative and driving for results – have long been thought of as particularly male strengths.'

A recent study by Saul Estrin and colleagues at the LSE suggests that men and women may place different values on the rewards they gain from work.[25] The study looked at the CEOs of 159 social enterprises in the UK. The gender pay gap was 29 per cent, higher than for the working population as a whole – yet these CEOs effectively set their own pay. However, the

---

25 Saul Estrin, Ute Stephan and Suncica Vujic, 'Do women earn less even as social entrepreneurs?', CEP Discussion Paper No. 1313, November 2014.

female CEOs had higher job satisfaction than their male counterparts. It would seem the female CEOs were more willing to accept a lower salary in return for more of the non-monetary benefits that enhanced their well-being.

Is it them?

Here is only a very slightly exaggerated account of a conversation overheard between two senior partners from a distinguished professional services firm:

Roger: Gerald, where do all our women go?

Gerald: I don't know, Roger.

Roger: I mean, we hire quite a lot of them. Very bright they are too, some of them.

Gerald: Very bright...

Roger: But then, you know, they just don't seem to stay. They go.

Gerald: They go...

Roger: I wonder why that is. Do you wonder, Gerald?

Gerald: I do, Roger, I do.

It feels like a *Bremner, Bird and Fortune* sketch. Except that the reality is not funny. To be fair to Gerald and Roger, they were at least asking some of the right questions. They seemed to recognise that something was amiss. They weren't quite sure what it was, and they certainly didn't have the first idea what to do about it. But they had noticed. And that is better than not noticing or, worse, pretending that there isn't a problem at all.

And the source of this problem does not, by and large, or at least in the first instance, lie with women. As Avivah Wittenberg-Cox, consultant and author of *Why Women Mean Business*, has said, we don't have to fix the women. Women's networks and support groups do help, and can encourage people to achieve more. But in a sense they are aimed at the wrong people. Women are OK. It's the men we need to do something about.

Why are men, in effect, keeping women out? Are they doing this deliberately or unconsciously? Why do men so rarely discuss the issue?

Maintaining the status quo is the easiest fall-back position. Remember that most large organisations will have originally been founded and run mainly by men and, as we have seen, most positions of power are still occupied by men. So it is no surprise that the values and culture of an organisation, and how it is structured and managed, tend to reflect that legacy – sometimes even when there have been genuine (well-intentioned) attempts to make the organisation more welcoming and thus more diverse.

What can men do differently to make businesses and organisations healthier environments in which more women can succeed?

It has long been a cliché that 'if you do not measure it, you cannot manage it'. And yet some businesses remain slow to collect useful data on what you might think are basic questions: who their staff are, how much they get paid, how often they get promoted and what they think.

An opportunity to use company law to drive up standards was lost when the previous government scrapped the proposed Operating and Financial Review before it had even come into force. Since October 2013, companies have had to prepare a narrative strategic report and this may encourage businesses to collect and publish more data on what, after all, is many firms' most important asset.

Where data does reveal problems and imbalances (and opportunities!), firms need to act to address them, which may include active sponsorship and mentoring of younger women executives.

Thought also needs to be given to so-called 'softer', cultural issues. Forty years ago, the academics Chris Argyris and Donald Schön explained that there was a difference in organisations between what they called 'espoused theories' and 'theories in use'. In crude terms: there is a difference between what people say and what they actually do. So companies may have admirable mission statements, codes of conduct, HR policies and all the architecture of career planning and support. But does any of it make any difference? Are they simply statements of impossible ideals? Do people act on them? Does anything change? That is what has to be measured. Corporate leaders need to be able to distinguish between their espoused theories and their theories in use – because their employees certainly can tell the difference between Stork and butter and, if they do not like what they see, many (of both sexes) choose to vote with their feet.

Another aspect of organisational culture that can act as a barrier to the progress of women has been described by the psychologist Edgar Schein as 'artefacts': the visible symbols of how that culture manifests itself. It could be a question of car parking spaces, executive washrooms, company cars, career coaches and so on. People at work notice these things and draw their own conclusions about where the business's priorities lie.

I recently heard about one big company that was struggling to understand why women found it an inhospitable place to work. Aside from some of the familiar problems, such as lack of flexibility and visible role models, there was the small matter of golf. The company loved golf – or at least its male bosses did – so 'golf days' became a standard way of offering rewards and incentives. The thing was, women never went or got invited … not even the women who actually liked golf! You can imagine the effect this had on female morale.

Artefacts may not have been consciously chosen – or, at least, they are not always chosen with knowledge of, or thought given to, the meaning employees attach to them. They are part of the 'clubbable' ethos: clubs include some people, but keep others out.

The media treat women in public life differently from men. This can be seen most clearly in the scrutiny given to women's appearances. Ann Widdecombe is quoted as saying, 'I have probably had a lot more comment about my circumference than John Prescott has had about his circumference.'

I felt the same way when I spent some time in the public eye going to court in the mornings in early 2013 and being very conscious that how I looked mattered hugely – so I perfected a smile and made sure I wore co-ordinated and smart clothes, as I knew they would be commented upon. The *Daily Express* had a close-up showing my long earrings, speculating on their value, as they looked like crystal – were they a wedding anniversary present from my husband? They were in fact plastic and had cost me 99p at a shop near Trafalgar Square. But to look less than smart is seen as tantamount to not asking to be taken seriously; it's taken as a sign that you are not in control, and people judge you for it – much more so for women than for the men.

Dame Fiona Woolf, who in 2013 became only the third female Lord Mayor of the City of London out of a total of 686 lord mayors in its long history, championed the role of women during her year in office. She and I had worked together trying to privatise electricity companies around the world at some point in my career and I was delighted when she became Lord Mayor, as that represented a prominent role model for many women. In an interview with the *Evening Standard* as her year as Lord Mayor drew to a close, she recounted that while she was negotiating a corporate finance deal, she re-entered a conference room to find the men giggling as apparently they had spent the intervening period trying to guess her dress size – easy, she is the thinnest person I know. But imagine a room of girls discussing the size of men's suits. It just wouldn't happen.[26]

Politics feels like a contact sport, at least to this spectator. The style of performance also matters. Caroline

---

26   Nick Curtis, 'Who's afraid of Fiona Woolf?', *Evening Standard*, 11 July 2014.

Spelman, later Secretary of State at Defra in the 2010 coalition government, recalls that 'Patricia Hewitt was given an incredibly hard time in a parliamentary sketch about some multi-coloured jacket she was wearing'.

More famously, of course, we have seen David Cameron snap at opposition women MPs who irritate him. The most notable example was the occasion in April 2011, when he told shadow Chief Secretary to the Treasury Angela Eagle to 'calm down, dear' at Prime Minister's Questions, borrowing a catchphrase that the film director Michael Winner had famously used in an insurance advert some time ago. It was a wonderfully revealing moment of sexist condescension.[27]

Cultural and psychological transformation

Perhaps there is something different in the way that women portray themselves, their general confidence and the way they project their image. A lot has been

---

27 http://www.theguardian.com/politics/2011/apr/27/cameron-sexism-calm-down-dear, accessed 2 February 2015.

written about their supposed lack of push and how difficult they find it to ask for pay rises or promotions in comparison to men.

Suzanne Franks is Professor of Journalism at City University. In her 2012 publication *Women in Journalism*, she refers to a study by Frohlich & Holtz-Bacha which attributed the difficulty of girls getting jobs in journalism after graduating from journalism schools to the 'friendliness trap'.[28] According to that study, women studying journalism demonstrate good communication skills, but when it comes to looking for work, that trait holds them back as it means they are not being assertive enough to compete successfully for good jobs. Rather than the female characteristic of 'friendliness' being valued, therefore, it seems to be a disadvantage to getting on!

Melissa Benn, the education writer and author of *What Should We Tell Our Daughters? The Pleasures and Pressures of Growing Up Female*, summarised what

---

28 http://reutersinstitute.politics.ox.ac.uk/publication/women-and-journalism, accessed 2 February 2015.

needs to change in a recent article in the Huffington Post:

> If things are really going to change, including women feeling more comfortable in the corporate and public world, men need genuinely to share care of home and children, including agreeing to work part-time if necessary. Employers and government must devise policies that help both parents manage those periods in their work life when the demands – and pleasures! – of young children are at their most intense…

In other words, there needs to be a substantial reallocation of paid and unpaid work in many families. Fathers are increasingly taking advantage of some flexible working practices, such as flexi-time or varying start and finish times, quite often so they can be more involved with their family (such as being able to take children to school or being home before their bedtimes), but this does not extend to working part-time. The proportion of men working part-time is rising but this is mainly due to more under-25s and over-50s working part-time, and a lack of full-time jobs. In families with young children, financial pressures are likely to have a strong influence on the division of labour and encourage the lower-paid parent – more often the mother than the father – to reduce their hours. But the sum effect of individual decisions is to preserve the status quo. In contrast, if more career-minded men spent a few years working part-time, it may not be seen as career death.

And if you should ever feel that perhaps we really are starting to see glimmers of the change that we need to see, then you can guarantee that something or someone will come out of the woodwork to remind everyone that there's still a long way to go. UKIP MEP Godfrey Bloom was usually good value for a jaw-dropping quote or two – 'sluts' who didn't clean behind fridges, and so on.

And still moments arise that reveal how deep-seated some prejudices are. In December 2014, at Claridge's, when 35-year-old Louise Burns tried to feed her twelve-week-old baby while having afternoon tea, an embarrassing kerfuffle ensued. A waiter came over and asked Ms Burns to 'cover up', although as this was her third baby and Ms Burns was clearly a capable adult, it seems unlikely that her behaviour was in any way extravagant. Indeed, she posted 'before and after' photos of herself on Twitter, and arguably looked more ridiculous in the second one, in which her torso was covered with a napkin.

There followed seventy-two hours of traditional British media nonsense and overreaction, with politicians chipping in on all sides. Nigel Farage said that 'ostentatious' breastfeeding in public should be discouraged – so a marching band accompaniment is obviously out, then, but would a feather boa count as ostentation or not? Boris Johnson said that breastfeeding mothers should be 'discreet' – would wearing a kaftan in which you can conceal both infant and breast be sufficiently unobtrusive? Nick Clegg seemed rather more relaxed.

For me, this row symbolised the ignorance and lack of understanding that some men still have about women. Jeremy Clarkson declared in his *Sun* column that breastfeeding in public was to be avoided – in a paper that still prints pictures of topless women every day (except at the weekends when, you understand, children might see them).

Is it 'the system'?

Governments in the UK have tended to be wary of imposing too much regulation on organisations. Of course, there *is* a lot of regulation, because much of it is essential if we are to have companies that can be trusted and markets that work reasonably well and to the nation's advantage. But there has, in most cases, been a preference for a non-regulatory approach if one can be found, and 'light-touch' regulation where necessary. For the past thirty years or so, Conservative, Labour and coalition governments have all had parts of the government machinery specifically designed to challenge departments wishing to regulate and scrutinise existing and proposed legislation. The mechanics and language may vary between governments ('deregulation' versus 'better regulation', for instance) but the intent is the same.

Applied consistently and rigorously, these processes

are both necessary and desirable – who would argue for unnecessary legislation (except, perhaps, lawyers) or against better regulation? Yet the danger is we encourage a mindset that sees important aspects of business practice as off-limits for the state (or, at least, off-limits for the law).

The management data that a company collects falls into this category. Company accounts are, of course, mandatory and require data to be collected and audited. But this does not extend to the data that a company collects about its workforce (with the exception of the gender composition of its board – now mandatory in company reports!) and, as discussed earlier, in many cases they fail to collect useful data. This means that organisations do not have a clear picture of gender parity within their organisation, let alone understanding of where, how or why disparity occurs. It is the Roger-and-Gerald approach to management and it is perfectly legal.

Collecting – and publishing – data on pay differentials by gender within an organisation does not in itself remedy whatever barriers create differentials, and the data might require careful scrutiny to avoid coming to spurious conclusions. But it is still better than no data at all. Equal pay audits would provide a starting point for tackling the causes of pay disparities within organisations, yet the current government has decided not to enforce section 78 of the 2010 Equalities Act, which requires employers with over 250 staff to measure and publish data on their gender pay gap.

Instead, in 2011, the government launched its 'Think, Act, Report' framework, which encouraged firms to publish data on pay differentials by gender. The idea was that a voluntary scheme, within which businesses pledged to be transparent, would begin to erode the differences without the need to resort to regulation. In August 2014, it was revealed that 200 firms had signed up to the initiative but that only four had provided data on the gender pay gap. We need to recognise that sometimes the only way to get businesses to change is to tell them they have to change.

Similarly, UK governments have tended to take a measured and cautious approach to regulating employment. Caricatures of the UK labour market as unregulated are wide of the mark. The OECD's database of employment protection indicators does show that the rules governing individual and collective dismissals in the UK are the least onerous (to employers) in Europe but the UK also has a legal national minimum wage and regulations governing working time and many other conditions of employment, often arising from EU requirements. Nevertheless, where possible, governments have sought to avoid being overly prescriptive, giving space for employers and employees to come to their own arrangements.

This approach, promoting flexibility but underpinned by minimum standards, has worked well in many ways. The lack of legal restrictions means that people in the UK have more choice over when, how, where and on what terms they work than people in countries with more tightly regulated labour markets – provided they can find an employer willing to offer whatever it is they want. But the flip side is no general obligation on employers to accommodate employees who wish to change their working pattern (such as changing their starting and finishing times in order to take children to nursery). Although many (if not most) employees are able to reach an agreement with their employer, for some, a change of employer might be the only way to change working patterns.

An independent task force chaired by George Bain, now vice-chancellor of Queen's University, Belfast and formerly chair of the Low Pay Commission came up with a solution: the 'right to request'. Eligible employees were given a legal right to submit a formal, written request to their employer if they wished to change their working arrangements and they were protected from dismissal or other forms of victimisation for doing so. Employers were required to follow a simple process in handling requests and give all requests reasonable consideration, but they were allowed to reject requests for a number of reasons that included business or operational constraints. Crucially, while employment tribunals were allowed to act in cases where the procedural aspects of the law had not been followed, they were prevented from second guessing the employer's judgement provided it was not based on incorrect facts.[29]

The original legislation came into effect in April 2003 and it applied to all parents of children under six (or

---

29 In 2014, the procedural requirements were replaced by a general requirement to give all requests 'reasonable consideration'.

disabled children under eighteen) who had twenty-six weeks' service with their employer. The Labour government extended eligibility in stages to cover the parents of all children under seventeen as well parents who were carers of children aged eighteen and over in specific circumstances. However, it was not until 30 June 2014 that the right to request was extended to all employees with twenty-six weeks' service.

Giving employees a right to request – but giving employers the power to say no without being challenged in law – has legitimised flexible working while at the same time addressing employers' concerns about the impact on the running of their business. Surveys show that most requests formalised what had previously been informal conversations, but some additional requests were made. Employers typically accept 80 per cent or more of the requests they get. Indeed, the process sometimes encourages both employer and employee to explore how they can produce a win–win solution.

Introducing the right in stages may have been sensible in addressing employers' concerns but, in doing so, it had some unintended and unforeseen consequences.

The initial legislation privileged the parents of young children and disabled children over other employees, and subsequent extensions simply privileged more parents. BIS monitoring surveys have also consistently shown that mothers are more likely to take up flexible working options than fathers, especially part-time working. So employees who did not have the right to request before 2014, which included employees with care responsibilities for people who were not their children, may have drawn the conclusion that mothers were being given an unfair advantage in the workplace. Employers may have seen the same facts in a different light: the addition of the right to request was another potential headache associated with employing mothers. In addition, the staged introduction of the legislation may have encouraged a perception that flexible working was for mothers of young children rather than potentially of value to all.

Seen in this light, the extension of the right to all employees with the relevant service in 2014 is both long overdue and a potential game changer. Finally, the law treats all employees equally and this may over time reduce negative perceptions of flexible working.

Employees with eldercare responsibilities – a number bound to increase with population ageing – are put on an equal footing to employees with childcare responsibilities. Significantly, the most recent BIS Work–Life Balance Survey found that, when it came to take-up of flexible working, there was a much smaller difference between men and women who cared for adults than there was between mothers and fathers.

Part III

Part III

Quotas –
there is no alternative

'We may not like quotas,
but we would like what they'd do.'

– CITED BY CHERIE BOOTH AMONG OTHERS.

I N 2002, WHEN Patricia Hewitt was in charge of
the Department of Trade and Industry, she was
responsible for the government's Women and
Equalities Unit. Since her early days in politics, Patricia had been worrying at the problem of why women
were always treated on a different basis to men in the
workplace. The film *Made in Dagenham*, now a West
End musical, captures in dramatic terms the first great
campaign in modern times for fair pay for women doing

the same work as men – in this case at the giant Ford car factory in Essex in 1968.

So when she had the power as a Cabinet minister to do something, Patricia Hewitt commissioned an independent academic study to examine the causes of the gender pay and productivity gap. The analysis showed there were a number of factors explaining the difference in pay:

- One was that, historically, women were less qualified than men. Today, that gap is disappearing fast and women entering the labour market now are on average better qualified than their male counterparts, but it has taken time for this to catch up across the various working ages where gaps still remain.

- A second factor is that women on average spend more time out of the labour market and find re-entry difficult.

- A third factor is that women are more likely to work part-time. People working part-time have higher job satisfaction than people working full-time but there is a penalty in terms of lower earnings – even adjusting for hours – and lack of career advancement.

Together, these factors explained about 60 per cent of the pay gap. The remaining 40 per cent, though, was due to labour market segregation and other, unexplained, factors associated with being a woman, which may or may not include discrimination; those are explored further later on.

But the plight of women losing out in terms of work status and career due to motherhood, however enjoyable, is a serious one. As we have seen, women who have children often come back at a skill level below them. A response to the later BIS inquiry on Working Families found that almost half of women professionals who take up part-time employment when they have children move into lower-skilled jobs.[30]

There is no better way for an economy to fail to grow;

---

30 Working Families, 'Response to the BIS Inquiry into Women in the Workplace', November 2012, http://www.workingfamilies.org.uk/articles/pdf/article/444, accessed 2 February 2015.

indeed, it is suicidal for an economy that needs high skills to prosper and grow – and it is a waste of resources. It is also a terrible waste of human potential.

More worryingly, women sometimes even have to start afresh. Even in areas like journalism, where freelance and part-time work seem to be 'de rigueur', which appears to offer an easy way of keeping your hand in while having children, this is deceptive. A woman journalist, married to a distinguished columnist, told me that after leaving one of the main newspapers for a few years to raise a family, she was brought back to write obituaries. She was later allocated to organising events, but as the newspaper was cutting back on contractors, those opportunities disappeared. She then gave up. Her view is that unless you are already well known and taken seriously as a columnist before you have children, coming back afterwards is not easy.

In ninety years of the existence of the BBC there has never been a female director general. Other major news broadcasting institutions are male-run. Indeed, one area of life where on occasions you can almost smell the testosterone is the media – and the national press in particular. Excluding three early pioneers, since 1987 just fourteen women have been editors of national newspapers in the UK.[31]

Only one woman has edited a daily broadsheet ever in the UK and that was Rosie Boycott, who briefly edited *The Independent* between January and April 1998. In the red tops, we of course had Rebekah Wade (later Rebekah Brooks) editing *The Sun* between 2003 and 2009. Currently (early 2015) there are no female editors of dailies of any type except Sarah Sands of the London free paper the *Evening Standard* and Dawn Neesom at the *Daily Star*. There have, however, been more women editors of the Sundays: Rebekah Wade at the now defunct *News of the World* and, more recently, Patience (now Baroness) Wheatcroft at the *Sunday Telegraph*, besides Lisa Markwell, currently at the *Independent on Sunday*.

There are, of course, many celebrated women writers and columnists. Nevertheless, a much-publicised study in 2012 also showed that three-quarters of stories that

---

31 http://blog.jtownend.com/2011/06/03/a-very-short-history-of-female-national-newspaper-editors-in-the-uk/, accessed 2 February 2015.

featured on the front pages of newspapers were written by men. Research of bylines across a range of UK national newspapers in 2011 (Cochrane, 2011 and again in 2012) revealed that the average ratio of stories written by men versus women (or at least with their byline on them) was 78:22.

Meanwhile, Suzanne Franks reproduces in her book a tweet from journalist Josephine McDermott when the Prime Minister summoned the leading editors to discuss the Leveson proposals in December 2012: 'BBC News channel shows parade of white, middle-aged male editors arriving at Downing St, bar Sarah Sands. Cd that be problem with press?' I suspect we could all confidently answer this on that evidence with a 'yes indeed!'[32]

So, if women are excluded from the opinion-forming elites, why should we be surprised that the policy-forming elites take little interest in fairness for women in work? This imbalance in the media is particularly surprising given that women now outnumber men in

---

32 http://reutersinstitute.politics.ox.ac.uk/publication/women-and-journalism, accessed 2 February 2015.

active student journalism, if measured by the articles they write, and also in formal journalism courses at universities. Indeed, in the most well-established university journalism programmes, the figures for 2012 suggest that the ratio of female to male students was about two to one. Yet they seem in general to be finding it harder to get the jobs than their male counterparts.

There are of course a myriad of magazines and local papers where women fare better. But the barometer of equality has to be the national press, which is so instrumental in shaping public opinion – and there we fail.

We need to talk about discrimination

Discrimination can happen in all sorts of ways. There could be discrimination which is unconscious and bars women from certain positions because of unfair perceptions. Sex discrimination is illegal, but you can hide it as 'the face doesn't fit'. It can be manifested as ageism bias against women, which seems to be rampant in the visual media. On the front page of *The Guardian* on 8 November 2014 there was a picture of a beautiful-looking

Olenka Frenkiel, award-winning reporter, aged fifty-nine, talking about her BBC experience and saying, 'I saw guys my age thriving. Women were gone. I too was being rubbed out.'[33]

And indeed this seems to be a discrimination that under any other name would be illegal. Of course, older men are also insecure when they reach a certain age, but the same *Guardian* article refers to research conducted in 2013, which showed that of all broadcasters over fifty at the BBC, 82 per cent were men. Women had been eased out. Miriam O'Reilly fought an ageism case against the BBC in 2011 after claiming that she was unfairly dropped from the rural affairs show when it moved to a primetime Sunday evening slot in April 2009. She was then fifty-three. She told a tribunal that she was warned 'to be careful with those wrinkles when high definition comes in' shortly before she was dropped from the programme. She argued that for her, that 'was a reflection of the BBC's view that women on

---

33 Jane Martinson, 'Why I rejected gagging clause – BBC journalist', *The Guardian*, 8 November 2014.

TV needed to look young'. She told the tribunal: 'I do not believe that a man would be asked about his wrinkles, nor offered hair dye.' John Craven, sixty-eight, who was then the show's main presenter, kept his job.[34] At least Miriam O'Reilly won her case.[35] Many others may not bother trying. Since the introduction of payments for tribunals, the cases brought against employers have reputedly fallen by 80 per cent.

The BBC is not the only area where this ageism bias works against women. The *Guardian* article refers to Selina Scott, who sued and won damages against Channel 4 at the age of fifty-seven in 2007, and the case of Anna Ford, who left the BBC in 2006 aged sixty-two, according to the *Guardian* article claiming that she had been 'sidelined because of her age'. Jon Snow, her boyfriend decades ago, continues to present *Channel 4 News*. He will be sixty-eight in 2015. And while the BBC dumps women presenters on account of age,

---

34 http://www.bbc.co.uk/news/entertainment-arts-11696591, accessed 2 February 2015.

35 http://www.bbc.co.uk/news/entertainment-arts-12161045, accessed 2 February 2015.

the Dimbleby brothers soldier on. David Dimbleby carries on uncontested chairing *Question Time* at the age of seventy-six and his younger brother Jonathan Dimbleby, a mere kid by comparison at the age of seventy, continues to lord it at *Any Questions?* Anna Ford is quoted as saying, 'I wonder how these charming dinosaurs such as Mr Dimbleby and [BBC world affairs editor] John Simpson continue to procure contracts with the BBC, when, however hard I look, I fail to see any woman of the same age, the same intelligence and the same rather baggy looks.'

But even David Dimbleby has smelled the whiff of change in attitudes – or at least the need to be politically correct. He was quoted as saying to the *Radio Times* in November 2013: 'Why should age matter with women? Women mature elegantly and better than men, very often. I don't think age should be a factor for women appearing on TV. I agree that it is demeaning to women and … it's a crazy loss of talent.'[36]

---

36 http://www.bbc.co.uk/news/entertainment-arts-22682588, accessed 2 February 2015.

In his view:

> There is a section among television executives who are always being hammered – quite wrongly in my view – to get the biggest possible audience, and they are told attractive young women will bring in a bigger audience than less attractive, older women – to say nothing of less attractive older men, like me...

And yet it has taken a long time for the first woman to be appointed as chair of the BBC Trust, which finally happened after Lord Patten resigned due to ill health after the Jimmy Savile scandals. That role has now gone to Rona Fairhead, ex-head of the Financial Times Group. It may not be deliberate policy to have gone for someone like oneself in the past – after one's own image, i.e. a man – but instead could have been the result of what is termed 'unconscious bias'. As Pryce, Ross and Urwin observe in their 2015 book *It's the Economy, Stupid*, 'some of the most important original theories of discrimination were primarily focused on behaviours arising from "conscious" decisions of individuals to discriminate between groups'.[37] One of the main economic frameworks used for understanding how discrimination works was developed by the Nobel prize-winning US economist Professor Gary Becker.[38] The way it manifests itself is by discriminating employers perceiving (often wrongly, one assumes) the cost of hiring a worker of a different (minority) group as being higher than the actual cost. These approaches, particularly in economics, as the Pryce book explains, 'assume that individuals from certain groups have a conscious "taste for discrimination", in that they purposefully and openly dislike individuals from other groups and act to avoid them in social and workplace settings'. This is an assumption that seems particularly unpleasant but unfortunately, in many cases, accurate.

That is, of course, thankfully declining as norms change. One of the most important developments in the years since Becker's work is the recognition of

---

37 Pryce, Ross & Urwin, *It's the Economy, Stupid: Economics for Voters* (Biteback Publishing, 2015).

38 For instance, Gary Becker's PhD thesis, 'The Economics of Discrimination' (1957).

'unconscious bias' – as opposed to the idea that individuals consciously dislike one or more groups within society. What we saw during the 1980s and '90s was a series of high-profile cases that fundamentally changed the nature of the discrimination debate in the UK. It became obvious that discrimination could just be the result of institutional systems and processes that are entrenched and in their nature serve to perpetuate discriminatory practices – even in situations where individuals may not necessarily have a conscious 'taste for discrimination'.

These cases pointed to the possibility that where discrimination exists, and under certain circumstances, individuals and institutions may in fact be discriminating but be genuinely unaware that they are doing so. They feel that they try very hard to overcome any personal bias when faced with job applicants from a variety of backgrounds; they treat all employees equally and use the same language with all. The Macpherson Report after the Stephen Lawrence murder and others showed that this is not enough, nor even appropriate. The manager who believes he or she is being fair to all and non-discriminatory because 'everybody gets invited down the pub after work, no matter what colour, sex, age, religion…' misses the point.

People's needs differ in a diverse society. Those with caring responsibilities, particularly women, as is more often the case, will not be able to join in and that needs to be recognised. Otherwise they will feel excluded not valued, and performance will suffer, with negative impacts on an organisation's performance. Dame Sally Davies, the first female to hold the post of Chief Medical Officer for England in its 165-year history, said in an interview with *The Times* in December 2014 that she 'had missed out on networking in the pub with male colleagues'. The habit of (mostly male) City workers entertaining clients in lap dancing clubs, apart from being abhorrent, also means that female professionals are unable to network as effectively as their male colleagues, and that can hinder promotion and success. Of course, one answer is that the clients should themselves be female so that those entertainment possibilities do not arise. But that may take too long!

In the meantime, therefore, more effort needs to go

into overcoming these unconscious, built-in biases so that we can have more equal and more productive societies. It is true that things have moved on from the days when a woman could only be seen as a sex object – or not be seen as all. A recent article in the *Daily Mail* reported a reduction in sexist language used to portray women. But it all just smacks of paying lip service to what is now politically acceptable and unacceptable to say; at the same time we have seen a huge increase in internet porn and degrading images of women continuing in all sorts of media outlets. Similarly, at work, firms are trying hard not to discriminate against women, at least on the surface. I was struck, though, by a quote in an article by the author of *High-Octane Women*, Sherrie Bourg Carter, which I reproduce below: 'Women in today's workforce … are experiencing a much more camouflaged foe – second generation gender biases … work cultures and practices that appear neutral and natural on their face, yet they reflect masculine values and life situations of men.'[39]

---

39 Grayson Perry, 'Default Man', *New Statesman*, 10–16 October 2014.

This, as I have outlined before, can in fact turn out to be just as much of a barrier to women moving up the promotion ladder as the previous direct and legally allowed discrimination used to be.

'Unconscious' discrimination can at times be wider and more sinister than that, demonstrated by cases brought by female workers against their employers in low-paid areas where women are 'ghettoised', such as cleaning and catering. In the eyes of the law, discrimination occurs if you are paying someone differently for the same job and if you are paying people different rates for a job with 'equivalent value'. The Fawcett Society quotes *The Guardian*'s October 2014 coverage of the Birmingham City Council workers' case against the council as follows:

> This case involved a group of 174 former Birmingham city council employees – including women who worked as cooks, cleaners and care assistants – who demanded compensation as they believed the council made bonus payments to men doing work graded at the same level, such as road cleaning and refuse collecting. Under a

bonus scheme, predominantly male refuse collection staff sometimes received up to 160 per cent of their basic pay. In one year a refuse collector took home £51,000, while women on the same pay grade received less than £12,000. Citing a breach of equal pay legislation, the Supreme Court ruled in favour of the 174 claimants in October 2012 and ordered the authority to pay out at least £757m in compensation.[40]

That represents a huge loss of earnings by women in society and it affects their opportunities and possibilities, and that of their children in their lifetime. The cost to the council was also, clearly, vast. A terrible waste all round.

Productivity, innovation, diversity

In the long term, our standard of living depends mainly on the rate of growth of labour productivity – how

---

40 http://www.mbsportal.bl.uk/taster/subjareas/hrmemplyrelat/fawcettsociet y/17062514timetoactgenderpaygap.pdf, accessed 2 February 2015.

much value we produce for each hour worked – and productivity growth has been far more important in explaining the dramatic increase in living standards in the advanced economies (and increasingly in emerging and less developed economies too). Many economists regard innovation – the adoption of new products, services, processes and ways of doing things – as having been the most important factor driving this productivity growth. These include Nobel laureates Edmund Phelps and William Baumol as well as Deirdre McCloskey and Robert Gordon, although (this being economics, after all) they differ in their explanations of why innovation was unleashed at the time of the Industrial Revolution and their expectations of whether it will continue to deliver productivity growth in the future.

Hence we need to consider how economic disadvantage for women might affect innovation and, thus, the future growth rate of the economy. This has been given less attention to date than the static, world-as-it-is costs, in part because it is more difficult to come up with meaningful numbers. Innovation can be a messy, sometimes chaotic-looking process and the creation of new sources of economic value can be accompanied by the destruction of existing value.

There are a number of reasons why greater employee diversity at all the different decision-making levels within an organisation facilitates and enhances innovation.

First, if a workforce is broadly representative of the current (or intended) customer base, it should prove easier to harvest insights across the complete range of customers about needs and wants, discovering how and why customers use the products and services and the improvements they would like to see made to them.

Second, diversity in its very broadest sense – incorporating not just gender, ethnicity and other differences recognised in equalities legislation, but also differences in background and personality type – can improve the quality of decision-making by reducing the risks of groupthink, which include premature rejection of options and over-estimation of the group's knowledge and control over events. Too much diversity can sometimes act as a brake; for example, if the task at hand is tightly specified and there is little, if any, choice over the means of achieving it, challenge from multiple perspectives can be wearing and slow the group down. A more homogeneous group may find it easier to trust each other because they tend to have more in common. However, because it is the difficult decisions that tend to matter most, diversity trumps conformity. This, of course, echoes the argument about why diverse company boards are superior to homogeneous ones, but it applies more widely to decision-making throughout the organisation. Mixing things up, and periodically refreshing how decisions are taken and who takes them, keeps organisations on their toes.

Third, many forms of innovation require highly advanced technical skills – or combinations of different skills and knowledge – that seem to change faster than education and training systems, which is a recipe for scarcity. For example, the video games industry looks for people with a flair for the creative side of the business, but usually allied with a strong background in computer science, mathematics and physics. When specialised labour is scarce, barriers to anyone realising their potential become more expensive.

Gary Becker regarded strong competition in labour and product markets as the best protection from employer discrimination. But while highly competitive markets will raise the cost of any barrier to human potential, they might not be enough on their own to eradicate these barriers. This is especially so when they have been created unconsciously or where they are seen as 'part of the way things are done in this line of business' and thus standard practice across competing firms. Challenge may then only come from a radical innovator who turns the business model upside down (and who may be an overseas competitor) – or from externally imposed change, such as quotas.

Can we do it better?

The truth is that many countries are implementing quotas. The new German government wants 30 per cent of all top posts to be filled by women. More advanced countries in this field, such as Norway, now find that quotas make sense. Norwegian companies and the economy haven't collapsed under the strain. France and Spain are also moving in that direction. There is evidence that organisations with diverse boards are, on the whole, doing better and are more profitable than those run only by men. One could dispute the way causality works – perhaps those companies that are already doing better are more relaxed regarding the risk of letting women loose on their boards. But it makes economic and business sense. Why not ensure that women, who tend to be the main consumers and decision makers on household spending around the world, are also involved in the drafting of the strategy and mission of companies serving them? And company boards should not be the only area of focus.

Quotas for executive positions in companies will encourage firms to engage in proper career progression and succession planning involving women; it will also encourage them to follow practices already successfully implemented in the civil service and in many business services firms that offer a family-friendly environment, even at higher levels throughout the organisation. It is vital that women (and the men who want to) can work flexibly, job-share if they wish and also get promoted while they are still on maternity/paternity leave.

How can we achieve a true meritocratic society?

What is obvious is that though women are employed in large numbers across many sectors of the economy, they are rarely represented in sufficient numbers in senior positions. There seems to be little justification for why women, who are just in a majority in this country, should be missing from so many areas that define what kind of nation we are. In addition, their absence is clearly starving the UK of the access to talent it needs to grow and prosper to its full potential. It also suggests that, far from the country being a meritocracy, the main winners are men of a certain type – the 'default man', as the artist and social commentator Grayson Perry, who delivered the Reith Lectures in 2013 has termed them in a leading article in the *New Statesman*.[41] White, heterosexual males of a certain class and background succeed because they are supported by a 'tribe' of men who see nothing wrong in elevating people after its own image. Left to itself, this is a classic example of a market failure:

---

41 Grayson Perry, 'Default Man', *New Statesman*, 10–16 October 2014.

there are costs to the economy if it is not addressed and the benefits, if it is, reach wider than the direct benefits to the individuals and the organisations involved. This therefore calls for proper intervention, building on the Equality Act of 2010, which would require businesses employing more than 250 people to measure and publish data on any gender pay gaps in their organisations to address that market failure.

Other than quotas, applied intelligently and flexibly, we see nothing else that might get us there in most working people's lifetimes. Dame Fiona Woolf, who had always declared herself not a great fan of quotas, is reported in the *Financial Times* of 15 January 2015 as saying: 'It's all taking too long. Why not have quotas for a bit?' Grayson Perry comes to the same conclusion:

> A move is happening ... but way too slowly ... I have heard many of the 'rational' (i.e. male) arguments against quotas and positive discrimination but I feel it is a necessary fudge to enable just change to happen in the foreseeable future. At the present rate of change it will take more than a hundred years before the UK parliament

is 50 per cent female …The ridiculousness of objections to quotas would become clear if you were to suggest that, instead of affirmative action, we adopted 'Proportionate Default Man Quotas' for government and business. We are wasting talent.

Conclusion

What do we want? Quotas!
When do we want them? Now!

WE DO NOT have enough positive role models for young women to learn from, to aspire to, and to draw strength and encouragement from. The lack of these role models is noted by women (and many men) and it is important because it can have a lasting influence. No matter how rational we aim to be, the choices we make depend on the information we possess about the world and how that works through to our thoughts, beliefs and perceptions.

If young women do not see other women occupying a fair share of senior positions in a particular profession, they will, for good or ill, draw their own conclusions – that it's too tough an environment in which to succeed, or that the men at the top don't want or aren't comfortable with the competition. Many will look for more welcoming career opportunities, and even those who do persevere do so in the expectation that, somewhere down the road, it's going to get tough.

But how then do we stop this from being a vicious circle (or one where progress towards equality might be so slow that the polar ice cap might melt first)?

Our argument is that the introduction of quotas (for a specified period in certain areas of business and public life where quick progress is both feasible and easily verifiable) could have a profound and lasting impact on public perceptions. Women would see a wider set of opportunities available to them and that would in turn affect the choices they make. After all, men have in effect operated a kind of quota system for themselves for generations, and that approach has served them rather well. Not surprisingly, the voices calling for quotas from City institutions, where women in senior positions tend to be seriously under-represented, are rising. The *FT* of

15 January 2015 quotes Karina Robinson, chief executive of the headhunting firm Robinson Hambro, as saying: 'My twenty-year-old self abhorred the very idea: my fifty-year-old self is adamant that without [quotas] progress is too slow.'

This is not *Nudge*-style behavioural economics. I don't think women's decisions about whether or not to continue on the career track are especially subject to the cognitive biases commonly identified in the behavioural literature. It seems rather that these choices are essentially rational given the odds women face in many careers. This is more of a shove or, perhaps more appropriately, a reboot of our expectations.

Has anyone cracked this?

A number of European countries have now introduced various forms of quota and Germany is set to follow suit in 2015. As we have seen, the Nordic countries lead the way in female representation on boards. All have quota systems of one sort or another and Norway is the only country where listed companies have managed to achieve full compliance with a stretching mandatory target – in this case, hitting 40 per cent board representation by 2009.

But men still hold most of the executive positions. In Norway, just 6 per cent of the top companies have female CEOs and the proportion of senior management who are female is just 18 per cent. Quotas are seen to have led to the so-called 'golden skirts' – women who hold multiple non-executive directorships – which is how Norwegian companies made the numbers up. As *The Economist* has pointed out, these countries have probably done more than anywhere else to provide women with equal opportunities, including generous maternity leave and first-rate, generously subsidised, state-provided childcare.[42]

Yet this does not seem to translate into very much higher shares of women in senior roles – with the exception of those company positions covered by quotas. Take the example of regulation and legislation that enshrines the right to paternity and maternity leave for men and

---

42 *The Economist*, 15 November 2014.

women. While it is right to legislate in this way, the costs to the employer in the short to medium term are not always fully appreciated and governments generally fail to compensate companies sufficiently for the increased uncertainty and costs that this implies. But, in truth, the bulk of this allowance continues to be taken up by women despite being available to both parents. This is well documented in research conducted by Catherine Hakim for the Centre for Policy Studies in 2011, which looked at experience of this in other countries that have legislated for shared parental leave by men and women.[43] Employers of course are well aware that this is – and will continue to be – the case, so women who are likely to have children in the near future are more likely to take time off and hence still more costly to employ, on average, than the men. Perhaps it takes time for the fundamental paradigm shift to materialise. But in the meantime the very aim of the legislation is undermined.

In fact, *The Economist* argued, this might be an

---

43 Catherine Hakim, 'Feminist Myths and Magic Medicine', Centre for Policy Studies, 2011, http://eprints.lse.ac.uk/36488, accessed 2 February 2015.

unintended consequence of this type of social policy. Generous maternity pay and leave arrangements seem to widen the experience gap between men and women because it means women take longer out of the labour market. Indeed, and in agreement with Hakim's analysis quoted above, in Sweden, where parental leave can be taken by either parent, three-quarters of the leave is taken by the mother, and to get to this stage, the Swedish government had to make the payments more generous and introduce use-it-or-lose-it 'daddy months'. (This, incidentally, means we shouldn't expect the introduction of shared parental leave in the UK to have much effect on who takes time off in children's early years.)

And when women in the Nordic countries do return to work, it is often on a part-time basis. While childcare is subsidised, high taxes and social charges can make hiring the domestic help that many women find they need to work full-time just too expensive.

Elsewhere in Europe, experience has been mixed. In most cases, legislation only applies to listed firms or the largest firms and there has been less progress in exempt firms. One general pattern has been, as seen in the UK, numbers on boards increasing to meet targets through non-executive rather than executive appointments. The easy way out.

One question that still has to be answered is whether creating a bigger pool of female non-executive directors, by law or voluntarily, will in time create an additional source of women for executive roles over and above those in the 'conventional' pipeline. The answer is, from evidence elsewhere, 'with difficulty'. The focus should not be on non-executive posts. Executive female positions would certainly be more useful, as they would at least be coming from within the organisation. The numbers would still be small and they wouldn't be making such a big difference to the way things are run. But that does not mean that quotas should be abandoned. Instead, they should be extended to where they would bite hardest – senior positions in organisations – as that is what will change an organisation's culture.

The penalties for failing to meet the quotas also seem to matter. In the Norwegian case, failure could ultimately have led to closure of the company. Laws introduced in Italy and Spain have had much less effect, possibly because of a lack of effective penalties (in the Spanish case, companies could lose favoured access to government contracts, but given the economic situation, this might not have been seen as a major loss). The French appear to have come up with a neat solution: if companies fail to meet the quotas, all nominations to the board become void and all directors lose their fees!

Intelligence required!

So any quota regulation, like any other legislation, would have to be applied intelligently to have the desired effect.

Very small firms must be excluded, as the costs would be disproportionately high and would undermine the very purpose of the legislation. A disproportionate amount of the burden of extra non-discrimination legislation can be borne by small firms, which are more likely to be creating job opportunities for disadvantaged groups who are otherwise excluded.[44] The firms

---

44 Peter Urwin, 'Self-employment, Small Firms and Enterprise', Institute of Economic Affairs, 2011.

that need to be covered are all FTSE 100 and all FTSE 250 companies further down, and also professional partnerships of a certain size, large private firms with over 250 employees, private equity firms that invest in many other companies, and all public sector organisations. It should also include Parliament and the government. It is unacceptable in a democracy and bad for the economy as a whole that important decisions such as voting on legislation and the running of our judicial system are left mostly in the hands of men, who, at best, represent only half of the population to whom these policies apply. It encourages misogyny and stifles the contribution that women can make to a fairer society that cares for the needs of all who live in it. But, equally importantly, it also hinders productivity and the growth of the economy to its potential.

But there is very little doubt that the benefit to society and the economy as a whole will be significant. As Sue Matthias, editor of the *Financial Times Weekend Magazine* and former chair of the pressure group Women in Journalism, rightly points out: 'A good and successful newspaper should reflect the society it's reporting on. If women are not in the fabric of the organisation, you've got a worse product.' And yet the *FT* is probably one of the most male-dominated newspapers around, despite Marjorie Scardino having been the first female CEO of Pearson, which owns it, between 1997 and 2012. And Sue's comments apply across all sectors. After all, women make some 70 per cent of all decisions on the household purchases of goods and services and yet are under-represented in the senior roles at the companies that produce them. After leaving Pearson, Scardino joined the board of Twitter, used by so many women, as its first female non-executive in 2013.

A cartoon in the January 2015 edition of *Prospect* magazine depicts a boardroom consisting of some twenty peacocks sitting round the table proudly displaying their feathers, with the caption underneath reading: 'We need to hire more women.'[45] Indeed they do. And if they did, the culture of the organisation would be subtly affected in myriad ways and the benefit would spread across all women who would feel that they could make

---

45 *Prospect*, January 2015.

an important contribution to the organisation. The spill-overs are significant. Although we have not focused on boards exclusively, the importance of bringing in a different attitude to the boardroom cannot be exaggerated.

Professor Sir Bruce Keogh, Medical Director of NHS England, argues that: 'Oestrogen dilutes testosterone in the boardroom and results in a productive endeavour.'[46] Better decisions can thus be made and the results for the organisation must surely improve as a consequence. There is also considerable evidence that the atmosphere in trading rooms in banks filled with high-testosterone males can lead to 'irrational exuberance', which less risk-taking females can temper. However 'trivial' that may seem, the wrong balance can make or break an organisation – or even a country. Men have traditionally gone to war, for example, much more happily than women – Margaret Thatcher perhaps being the exception! A greater representation of women in politics, particularly in the Cabinet, would surely result in women's voices being listened to more. For some time, until the

---

46 'Medical chief tells female bosses to play fair', *The Times*, 17 December 2014.

promotion of Nicky Morgan to replace Michael Gove in the summer of 2014, there were just three women Cabinet members: Theresa May, Justine Greening and Theresa Villiers.

Given that more than half of the electorate is made up of women, it seems odd that our top leaders do not directly represent that majority of voters. But these are just small examples of a series of classic market failures in most areas of the economy. There are large externalities to be gained if they are addressed. At present, the benefits from better gender equality are simply not priced properly in the decision-making of individuals and businesses. Left to itself, this situation results in a sub-optimal allocation of resources – the worst thing that could happen in economics. As things stand, this misallocation is keeping Britain back and costing us dear.

Sally Davies confessed she has succeeded because she is a workaholic and added: 'If you have a life as well, you aren't going to do as well.' Why should women who reach the top be exceptionally good when the man doesn't usually need to be? Even in areas where women are employed in large numbers, like NGOs, only 27 per cent of them are currently run by women. Barbara Stocking, the former executive director of Oxfam Great Britain, was quoted in an article as saying: 'We're being very complacent about this and we have to face up to it … How can we help women through the system … You can't do anything until you recognise that it's not going to work the way we're doing it.' And she added: 'There is this prime assumption that the men who are leading these organisations are really good. They're not … some are pretty mediocre. At the moment women are having to be very, very good to get to the top.'[47]

Indeed, as has been often said: 'I will know when women have reached equality when there are as many mediocre women at the top of the organisation as there are men.'

How can we make it work?

The cost–benefit calculation, therefore, as in any other

---

47 http://www.theguardian.com/global-development-professionals-net-work/2013/aug/01/women-in-leadership-international-ngos, accessed 2 February 2015.

policy area, suggests that government intervention of some sort is required to meet that market failure. What that intervention should be is of course the crucial question. Encouraging and cajoling can only take you so far. Changing this culture with some form of intervention, particularly through imposing quotas for women in senior executive posts, would speed the process through. A lot of progress has been made but we are still a long way from offering women a real equal opportunity in work. Waiting for the slow and painful process to sort itself out will take too long. And, as Keynes famously said, 'In the long run we are all dead.'

Quotas will benefit all women, not just the ones in senior positions, because of the trickle-down effect they will have. They will force firms and organisations to seriously think about talent pipeline and succession planning and to adapt working practices so they retain women rather than losing them once they have been trained. This will include introducing quality flexible work and part-time work at senior levels, aimed at keeping women in the workforce and ensuring they get promoted even if they don't work full-time for a while. Or thinking more innovatively about supporting childcare costs, which are a great impediment to women working full-time. It will become a business imperative. The signals of a wider employment opportunity will also affect educational establishments and eventually the career choices of women, who will gain confidence that they too could have the positions they want as the numbers of role models across a greater variety of sectors increase. This will also encourage greater competition for jobs and the pay gap will decline. Of course, women will always be able to make a choice about their lives, particularly when it comes to having a family. But it will make having children even more of a joy when the day comes when pregnancy doesn't signal the end of the prospect of a glittering career.

For the man, children, marriage and the security they bring propel him forward. For the woman, they keep her back. There is no way the current situation can be transformed except through legislation to fundamentally change society's norms of what is and isn't acceptable. And it should be unacceptable to discriminate against the majority of the population for the benefit of the minority. The cost–benefit ratio doesn't stand up to scrutiny. Quotas, like the legislation on wearing seatbelts, on drink driving, or even on banning smoking in public places, can change behaviour. What was commonplace one moment becomes frowned upon the next. Changes have to be made intelligently: they must be targeted to the right set of companies, they must ensure that cost is minimised, they must extend further than the boardroom and they must be applied over a significant period, taking account of different starting points in different sectors.

One may wonder: why targets only on women and not also on all other 'minority' groups? Well, women are in a majority, as it happens, so we might as well start with that. And quotas for women will hopefully make organisations more understanding of all forms of diversity (including race, disability etc.), which also brings strong business benefits, as so many studies on the subject have demonstrated. The civil service, as it happens, already has targets for minority groups, including in relation to disability and sexual orientation, and it tracks progress carefully.

Finally, to those – especially women who have succeeded – who say they are opposed to quotas because they want to be promoted simply on the basis of how good they are, not because of any positive discrimination, I would say that indeed, I am all in favour of true meritocracy. But you don't achieve that by excluding a huge part of the population from competing against you. Or by assuming that the rest are not as good as you are simply because they have not applied for those posts. The truth is that women have often felt compelled to go for the exit before getting even a sniff of the stairs that may lead up to the higher echelons of power. Many would have been discouraged from playing 'the man's game' to achieve success as the price is too high to pay, thus leaving the field open to just some of us 'queen bees' that Sally Davies alludes to. That is the opposite of meritocracy – and it assumes huge arrogance on the part of those who have made it. Are the many men, or the few women, who have succeeded really so special in relation to the rest of the population that they alone know how to run companies, chair meetings, invest our money? I doubt it.

After all, boys are in no way better than girls in general at school. If they excel in certain subjects, like science, it is often because the girls have been discouraged or turned off at a young age, often due to lack of female role models in these areas. Men don't get where they are by meritocracy alone, as they compete against a much smaller number of potential candidates than if women were equally represented across the board in all fields of the economy. And that is what the system in practice does. It effectively encourages a type of nepotism by subtly excluding so many women from positions of authority and from so many walks of life. The result is that we in the UK end up with a less talented, less innovative and less productive economy that costs us dear. Surely that can't be what we as a nation want or should settle for? Second best? Surely not!

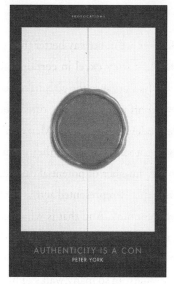

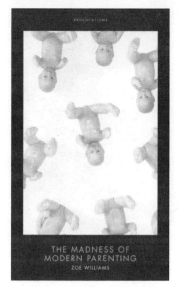